Poet Laureate of the English-Speaking World

by

Gary Kent Spain

poet-fiddler

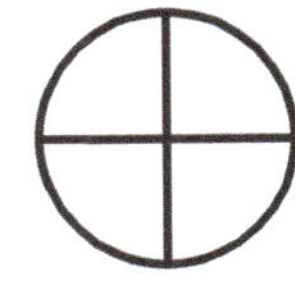

(and discoverer of the lost core of Kabbalah)

To
Brighid
Goddess
of
Poets
Healers
&
Smiths

Preface

There is simply no excuse for no-one having approached me ere now to appoint me such, so I have appointed myself. I have explored all types of poetry and most known forms, including the traditional Celtic forms in all their intricacy. I am not particularly accomplished at haiku (I offer a few), but real haiku is Japanese anyway.

It seems to me imperative that the English-speaking world *have* a poet laureate, as the quality of verse in the journals is extremely poor. The tribe (of English speakers) needs a druid to guide them as to what exactly constitutes poetry. If I cannot answer this directly, I can at least provide examples of many distinct kinds of actual poem so readers might choose for themselves what most appeals to them, then try and better it. I think I am most moved by intense free verse; yet I love reciting some of the stricter forms for their musical beauty.

English is the richest language in existence. It has way more words than any other. It combines down-to-earth Germanic with highfalutin French and Latin and Greek, with a bit of Celtic seasoning thrown in (half unbeknownst to OED). The main center of English-speak (the U.S.) shows a similar raking-in of complementary influences in its music (I presume in its art as well, though there I am no aficionado). We inherit much of Old World melody—from Irish to Slavic to African and Asian—plus the incredible advances in harmony-versus-dissonance since Debussy; add into the mix Afro-Cuban jazz and its incredible rhythms; and so on and so forth. Sadly the 'so forth' includes some lame stuff as well (like Philip Glass), but oh well.

The two great blossomings of song in my lifetime—poetry set to music, in its highest form—have been the age of the 'freak' or flower child, and the New Wave era. In the freak era, we sought inspiration in everything from antiquity to blues, from Troubadours to jazz: the goal, to open minds to the far greater extent of the real world than of the individually perceived worlds we were brought up to believe in. In the subsequent New Wave era, a band had to be quirky (or else just incredibly good, like the Police) to resonate, the result being a near parity between girl bands (or at least girl singers) and boy bands (or singers). I take inspiration directly from both eras, and from many ancient and modern poets—Sappho, Virgil, Taliesin, Caedmon, François Villon, Shakespeare (my earliest 'tutor'), Lovelace, Tennyson, Masefield, T.S. Eliot, Cummings, Ferlinghetti, to name but a few—as well as from some of the strict forms themselves, especially traditional ones (older the better), for their music and their challenge. I utterly shun what today's academics call poetry, which frankly is dull and stilted, sorely lacking in power and variety.

My only other skill is a well developed musical ear. I play Irish airs and jigs (plus a few reels, though without much skill) on fiddle and have written a hundred or more songs on guitar. I grew up playing classical violin. My father, the amateur actor and Shakespeare aficionado), who raised me on the Bard's plays, discussed poetic rhythm with me at length while writing his book *Shakespeare Sounded Soundly: The Verse Structure and the Language* (by Delbert Spain). He suspected my musical training might allow insights on the subject of rhythm that he lacked. It was my mother who had been the musician and played many instruments, including the pedal organ. (My dad, poor guy, was tone deaf, meaning he had no sense of pitch.) I consider my choice of parents this time round quite fortuitous. Yet neither skill has been very remunerative, although I confess I had an opportunity to make decent money at computer programming (like my father) but gave it up after a few years because I found I could not continue at it and remain a poet of any consequence. The two skills appear to fight over the same region of the brain.

Well, articulate as I tend to be in prose, it is poetry that offers *economy* of verbiage in stout measure. Hence *to* it.

G.K.Spain
16 February 2023

PS. I just noticed (2/4/24) the absence of anything herein utilizing the Spenserian stanza per se and realized at the same time that I actually have not read *The Faerie Queen*, which, on reading its first ten stanzas—*viii* and *ix* listing the poetic qualities of trees!—I realize is a must-read for me. My apologies to Spenser, whose sonnet form I did explore; it is just that I lack the patience to compose (or even sit through in its entirety) anything so epic as to merit such a fine stanza.

Table of Contents

P o e t

Songs Out of My Late Childhood

A Time of Great Awakening

The Ramifications

Workshop 'Gems'

Recent Stuff

T a n i s t

B a r d

Asian Poetry Forms

[Each poem is in the same form as the previous poem unless otherwise specified.]

Quantitative Meters (Greek & Roman)

Rowing Meter (Strong-Stress Alliterative)

Syllabic and Shaped

Traditional Welsh Forms

Welsh Measures Allowed the Chief Bard

In the Style of Dark Ages Britain

[Total: 375 poems]

Poet

A poet he will look you in the eye, his eyes a pack of hounds,
and make you see what you entomb and treasure in your tall mounds.

Windsong

Wind song
Eyes of the past
Judge what you see
Leave me the rest

Sad note
Sung for the trees
Bend of the boughs
Ache of the knees

Truth's Champion

Eyes, stand with the poets of an elder age
Against the sprawling currents of the lesser fields
That rampage over times present and counted on,
Where deeper shadows lie. And champion the man
Against the herd, eternity in place of time,
The unseen rather than its vague appearances.

Surprises not that others stick their forks at us
And prod us with their voices like a steaming iron
Come to take the wrinkled edges off my mind.
Their own wrinkles are labeled folds and then paraded
Before us as examples of the smooth: I balk
At such deceptions. Why not call things what they are

And leave the rest to others.

My Vista

I see life
From the underside,
From the bottom up
    Like a tree.

I see life
As eternal pain,
The eternal pain
    In me.

Songs
Out of My
Late Childhood

Phantoms

Phantoms touched him in his lonely hours
and stabbed him in the midst of troubled sleep,
telling him of the joys that he had missed.
They drove him slightly mad recalling those
who'd made him what he almost failed to be
and wishes now he weren't.

Steeple

A steeple, and I asked him how he felt—
a tall white steeple—and he said he feared
that he would fall. But then he said he wished
he *would* fall someday, before the sky
pushed him down.

(Two Flawed Elegiac Couplets)

Non apprendi illas elapsas quas cupiebam
Nam timeo tactae ne mutent illae
Ne tactu vulgetur caritas et dubito aevum
Vulgatorque aevo caritas ignavo.

As Sophocles Sang His

I have found a tragedy
that cannot be sung
as Sophocles sang his.

I have found a pathos
beyond the tears of Jove
that Apollo could not sing
with all the spilled voices
of his worshipers
had he a hundred
clouds to climb
like his native Olympus
(or as his splintered rusting remnants
rotting on the aftermath of agony would say . . .)

I have found a tragedy
that Troubadours would envy
though it most certainly lies
beyond their skill.

And where a poet
might have sung it
with lyre-plucked sweetness
once sung
it's hardly worth the canvas
whereon it sits
sung.
Tragedy which in its very utterance
vanishes.

It is not purple.
It has no Olympian grandeur
with which to dignify itself
for by being Olympian
grand and dignified
it lacks the very quality
that makes it sad.

And now that it has been announced
with all due clearing of throats
I hear the usher laughing.

A painting is never quite as pure
       as what it paints.

A painter is never so pure of heart
       as the people he paints.

I still remember tragedy
in its crisp realness
before it spilled out of my tongue
and into song.
I remember it
as once proud mother-lovers
unable to be proud anymore
unable to be sung anymore.

Deorc−land

The clouds hovered, black vultures in dim light
A wingspread of endless miles to each
The sun covered, the sun blotted out
The wind, it was . . . ever . . . dead.

We moved fast
And wind blew
Against our faces

And stirred her hair
Harping pleasant discords on her
Pleasing to me
Wind blew
A synthetic wind, as we moved
Yet not empty.

The dark clouds still hovered
Devouring the sun of no-longer memory
      There is no sun in Deorc-land
The wind, it was . . . ever . . . dead
Powerless to propel the clouds
Powerless to drive them away
The dull, heavy, lead clouds
Smothering the sun.

And we moved faster
Wind-craving
And wind blew furiously
It battered us
It stirred
Her hair
Harped discords
On the strands of her hair
Pleasing
To me
      There is no sun in Deorc-land
In Deorc-land.

The wind, it was . . . dead
It touched only us
As we moved in bas relief
To the rest of men
Who just wait
In the black land, the dark land
Deorc-land.

Poet's Apology

i know the laugh
that comes out of an impatient ear

and i have seen serenity
perched on the brow of a madman
and smiles painted on the masks
of ancient comedy and modern smugness

and the existentialist grin is always
staring me in the face

i know it's foolish to prolong
moments into memories
or caution into fear
and i know the laugh
that comes out of an impatient ear
          yet still i am verbose

and is it pompous
to make a sort of music out of words?

and is it pompous
to cast my feeling
into the statue
of human language?

for i myself have laughed the laugh
that comes out of impatient listening
and it still seems fitting
that though i might express a feeling
with a few simple chords
that feeling overflows
into explicitness
and pompous
verbosity

Sonata Adagio

A speck of dust
caught up by a writhing red-striped snake
A human entity
mirroring two hypnotic red dots
    A pair of flaming eyes
    searching endlessly and relentlessly into the mind of the man
    finding nothing
A thinking man
without a thought

    A thousand bleeding pin-pricks
    augmented by a single piercing wound
    A siren
    chilling war-cry of a fleet-footed rodent that challenged the writhing snake
A thinking man
with a thought
a reflection
what household is in pain this night?
    Again the siren
    cry of anguish in retreat
    cutting off the reflection as a pebble in a glassy pond

A proud human entity
bathed in the fading glory of a single passing thought
A man in a moving cage of steel
mirroring a pair of eyes
    Hypnotic omniscient eyes
    undeceived
    unchanging
A speck of dust
falling off the writhing red-striped snake

A speck of dust

Progress

Dappled grey
grazing under an old oak tree—
a car streaks past in a blaze of sunlight on steel
and cloud of exhaust . . .
        the car is faster.

Old foxhound,
lying on the living-room floor—
"Put the dog out and turn the television on
out in the den, honey . . ."
        the TV's more loyal.

The dappled grey and the foxhound
look back longingly on the hunt
through a veil of noise and idleness.

Boiling Brew

You animal of the soft twitching limb,
Thing of warm smiling and of mermaids near,
Teach me to love as others love and hear
As others hear who listen to each whim
And calling of their blood. Teach me to swim
The smooth swift currents of a thing held dear
And in that liquid touching drown the fear
Of one still standing on the ocean's rim.
Thing of bright walking on a dismal land,
You have in me a cauldron's boiling brew
Waiting to be poured out into the sea.
Spill me and I will do what lovers do
And warm the waters where you swim with me
And love you till we wash up on the sand.

Mocking Bird

The mocking bird is gone tonight
where I walk among the trees
looking for him.
Winter is here and he is gone
though I expected him to be here
singing his merry thoughts to me
as he sang them to me
a month or two ago.
There isn't any snow
to tell me that winter
has taken him from me.
Perhaps if I could understand
the language in the wind's chill
I'd hear him whispering,
"Wait, I'll be back.
Wait, I will come again
to cheer you when you walk in poet's madness
to hear me when you ought to be asleep.
While I am gone, wait
and I will sing to you again
and I will sing again
will sing again."

A Time
of Great
Awakening

After experiencing synthetic mescaline (the real stuff) and some acid, I dropped out in my third quarter at Dartmouth—which devastated my parents, me being an only child and all—and became a real person.

Blacksheep

I am the black sheep. I love not the flowers.
I love the green of grass and forest firs.
Take back your pillars and your mighty towers.
Give me a tree that bends when a breeze stirs.

Invocation

Children of Adam, climb to where the demons
Jump in abrupt obedience to gleemen
    Who sing in the night.

Gods of Olympus, shiver in my wake
And I will show you where whole worlds do quake
    For fear of your might.

To the Muse

O goddess of a thousand shining masks,
You answer only poets when they ask
To taste of but a single endless sip
Of the transcendental wine
　　　That dances on your lips.

Waters of World

Waters of world
ask me to swim with the grace
of leopard sharks
and I can only stand bewildered
and think the other creatures of the sea
are all as lost as me

Chaos is strong
waiting as I on the brink
trouble to think
suck me along that eerie wave
that loses all its dullness in the sun
and crashes on the sand

And if I fall
cover the place of my death
with shining waves
and flowers of the seaweed fine
for all the other creatures of the sea
who are as lost as me

Death of Solemnity

As one who walks gravely
through scenes of mad celebration
and wears his purple grandeur
in the squinting of his eyes
while puppets play around him

as one such sad-textured
plaything of the wind
I have stood on my rock
wearing tinted glasses
during the day
and smiling as if smiling
were nothing more than the proper thing to do.

But blindly stand I not once more
upon that self-same rock and stage
whereon unseeing in his rage
stood someone similar to me
        not long ago.

        And where before
my stage seemed cluttered
        by the clamoring movement
of toy-mad puppets
        who tottered from strings
like reflections of a thousand kites
or kites flown by the sky, their strings now seem
to vanish in the stratosphere as in a dream
of distant purple grandeur:
        now there's room
for all the puppets you can fly
in my huge corner of the sky.

O bright blue limitless soaring seas
of peppermint rising over wintergreen,
more beauty bounces on your whispered breeze
than shouting men have ever seen.

Language

Wind, why do you carry
the pompous chatter of mankind
upon your great highway?
These words that furless mammals
cough into the air
are like some chemist's artificial brew
devised to give false sense of majesty.
We think ourselves worthy of laziness
because we have our tongues
with which to make excuses for ourselves.
Why, wind, must you play
a part in this conspiracy?
Methinks you have no love of laziness,
so why do you blow men's words to me?
You who touch all things,
why do you aid the cause of untouching
and help men send illusions of themselves
across the air?

Colors

In weathertime were proud birds
that beat their wings against the sky
long ago when unseeded rainstorms
still dwelt on the earth

They were the ancestors of sparrows
who speak to us in high shrill tones
melodies that echo
their ancient tongue

In the end every species
must inevitably see the world
as such a tiny simple thing
just tinkering with it loses all its glamour

And so they make of it
a single vast plaything
a huge canvas on which to sprinkle
colors as the birds have done

Flowers

I don't like flowers
that are kept in rows
so loudly do they stink of order
that they must be kept in fenced back yards
so as not to be trampled upon
by uncivilized pedestrians.

I love the weeds that proudly disfigger
the fragile world of the botanist and bulb-buyer
who crops his hair in echo to the sport
he has with his hedges:
clip, clip, and the branch is gone
that dared to surge beyond his well-planned lines.

I don't like flowers
that are kept in rows
nor the rows in which men
are marched to their untimely end.

Acid Trip

Risin' tide
Came right up by my window-side
And spilled across the beams
Of its wooden frame
Spewing forth archetypes
Dim shadows of an elder age
Like ripples of its maker's rage
Smeared on the tapestry

And staining its unblemished pride
With angles of view
Transformed upon the great eternal stew
Through cataracts of wonder
Into a braid that trickles under
Everywhere I cast my eyes
Trying to be wise.

Le Passé Simple

It all has to do with time
like antelopes
and bears in winter

the bear who waits
for something to resolve itself in anger
a residue of ages past

and the antiquated antelope
answers in the afterworld of dew
where the deer dances
like dew upon the sun's rays.

Where does it all lead?
to the laughing liaison
of mind and the matter at hand?

Is it mind over matter
or matter over mind?

The answer is neither
or else we are all blind
to the love-throngs of beauty
and the balance of time.

Flower Child's Humble Plea

O ancient one,
you that wear the mask of the sad side of Thespis,
how can the dancing of the leprechauns
in the wee hours before the next dawn
not unfasten that mask of chains?

Wise old patriarch,
father to the brazen statues of power
whose shadows are our darkness,
how can the laughing of bright-eyed babies
waiting for the trumpet rays of a new sun
not shatter your bronze progeny?

O sculptor of frowns
that have it not in you to laugh,
your statues ape the mask you wear
and hide the sun with all their care
and make the babies weep
to see their cold grey stare.
Come, o great frowning elder,
come, kiss awhile
that we may melt your frowning mask
into a magic smile.

Legend of a Dope Fiend

Lump of fat and ball of ire
sitting in the corner there
watching the last flickers of a fire
absorbed into the air

And if you chance to see him
in the corner of your eye
watch as the last flickers die
and if you chance to see him
ask him why

Flame of once impressive hue
burning in the corner there
pity you took so little time to do
and take so long to die

Fire burn and fire flicker
its shadows are uncertain and aghast
Devils on the ceiling snicker
the pale delight of dying shadows cast

And if you chance to see him
    ask him why

Conscription

Than suns which rise
    over the riddled tidbits
of man-game on his maiming-ground
    no morning-beams seem brighter
than suns who return
    from when as targets they lived
to fight the wars of presidents
    and of princes unloftier
than suns. And I wonder
    if women's tongues will always
seem to bid that I whet them
    for they beckon more sweetly
than drums which tread
    their trill-tearing path
across the years of my youngness
    which yearn for one woman more
than for any blood-won
    battleground of war.

Song of Revolution

Sloppy politicians
with your sly grins of caviar
and all the great giants
that you serve

syndicate and president
the tilted poles
imposed at either end of the world
in your twisted fashion

it's only a shadow any more
imposed by lines that blur the sphere
of the real world
in your twisted fashion.

O beauteous one that show thy thighs
in soft stockinged ways
I am waiting. And o thou
Mighty Mouse of flannel . . .

There's scarcely a higher thing than mind
so let it not be said
we gave our fellow minds the brush
and left our lovers dead
        in our cold century.

It's only a shadow any more
that keeps your unstockinged beauty from my eyes
and keeps us from warming
ourselves on each other
        in our cold century.

Half Madness

Another year has seen its dawn
though New Year's hasn't happened yet

and suddenly my love-struck brain
is awed by time.

The body has revolted from its master
leaving the mind
to fend for itself
in uncertain substance.

Upwards I drift
like hydrogen or helium.

Can helium – The Priestess –
be only a mirage?

My priestess she's a substance still
a dream remembered unfulfilled
and perhaps as yet undreamt of
in Solomon's philosophy.

And I am but a dog of time
though I have been a bristling pig
in times before the spear's point
was made of brass.

Idylls! build ye idols to a king
who sees his substance as his crown?

He will lead you falsely
always falling down.

But my tongue will tell you truly
of the things which I do know
things that to his eyes
might not even show.

Mark me well, you ungrateful wench:
you're all I want to hear and feel
and talk to in my afternoons.
Your love is everything to me,
though I am nothing but a dog of time.

Song of the Enchanted Ones

Shift your feet upon the pavement.
Shift your feet and use soft voices.
Shift your feet and wag your tongues
      While the great ones are deciding.

Twiddle, twiddle, play your fiddle,
Shift your feet and feed your middle:
The great ones think while you are young
      And die when you are old.

And in the far-off reaches
Of Mordor and of mountains,
Dark dwarves and hairy half-men
Are moving and are restless:
They pass the ways that shadows pass
With purpose in their eyes
      (In Mordor, they are very wise).

These dark shapes are among us.
They shift their feet among us.
They wag their tongues among us,
Soft voices in our midst.
      (The great ones bare their teeth and frown.)

And in the past we wander
And frolic in the future
And make the great ones tremble
And quake with fear to see us,
We shadowed shapes that sneak about
And sharply whisper "why"
In Mordor, where the shadows lie.

Twiddle, twiddle, play your fiddle,
Shift your feet and feed your middle:
The great ones think while you are young.
      When you are old they die.

The Three Norns

[in my own form, called Trapeze[*]*]*

weave the strands of everything
together
and apart again
together where they meet in ashes
and fall apart in rising gases
scattered by the wind
together
where the roots of trees become
trunks
bent down by strong gusts
together as men come together
only to wage
war
and dedicate their carcasses to breezes
together
as when you and I
come together for a while
and part again tomorrow
remembering in sorrow
how we loved

weave the strands of everything
together
and apart again
weave while angry men
unravel
the tapestry of ages

---

[*] (consisting of lines of symmetrical stress-pattern)

Deepen Wide

the mind rises
in springs and in mountains
gurgling its way
through rocks and through pebbles
and through the soft soil of earth-world
a thousand and a thousand
water-wanderers
that meet in creeks and in streams are flowing
and make a river
deep and wide
that washes to the sea
as raindrops carve their way to puddles
here and there

Old Cat

How now, old cat,
sitting betwixt my thighs,
what have you to tell?

Have you a brave omen
to send me on my way?

Prick up thine ears
and tell me the tales
that travel on the wind.

Have ye a hearty purr
to send me on my way?
Prick up thine ears
and tell me what the breezes say.

Hymn to Love

Each poem is a mystery
That cannot be unraveled in a day.

The music on the lips of time
Could never be contained within one lay.

And yet, each song I sing for you
Contains the germ of everything I feel.

You are the muse that drives me on.
You are the only god to which I kneel.

January 1ˢᵗ, 1972

The hours of daylight,
        the dancing visions
and their tongues foretelling,
        tread on my eyes
in sing-song patterns
        of celibate horsemen
and candied apples
        covered by the sands of time.
And their tongues' drippings
        and their talk of dabbling
in fancy tomorrows,
        mighty though they sound
these hopes of having
        come headlong falling
like all dreams of lofty things
        that have no leg to stand on.

The Hood of Night

Blood runs its swift, unswallowed course
Thru vein of dog and deer and horse
And thru man's magic manikin
When mated with a woman's skin.

But wanting something sundrous and aloof,
Man runs in circles round and round and round.

The hood of night is tightly drawn
In limbo, where our ways have gone,
Over the grave unmoving face
Of time and place.

The hood of night covers her face
Where she is walking, softly stepping
Upon the web woven by night
For her to spread her spider legs upon.

And something in the whisper
Of blood as it rushes
Continually turning
Breathing into life
Makes time eternal
Object immaterial
And presence known to be devoid of place.

Over-Intellectualized Romance Blues

I feel like I'm retiring
    into the tinsel cage
of talking like a guru
    or a gilded sage
pretending to wisdom
    like a teacher in school
when I'd much rather play the simple fool.

I seem bent on the burdensome
      and unbearable task
of cackling out answers
      to the questions you ask.
Oh please, can this ritual
      of reasoning end?
I've got a little wound I need to mend.

Tickled

Serammerass Sir Runamuck
came eye to I with a gentle duck
and thought he was standing upside down
when suddenly the duck became a clown
and wiped away his tears
compounded out of many painful years.

In simulated combat
they chatted for awhile
and in the end Sir Runamuck
learned how to smile.
But it took a long lesson
to lessen his longing
an' 'e ain't cured yet:
you see, he's more tickled than pickled.

Uneasy Contentment

A little girl from down the block
      Has fixed me in her spell.
I've scratched my head upon a rock
      And only the years will tell.

It strikes me in sundry ways
      How similar we are
Although we have our separate ways
      Of seeking the same star.

Announce the roar of cannon at her feet
    If you can conceive
      Of such ballroom delicacies.
It's as if she walks inside the breeze
      That tumbles all about my hair.
She's always there in one form or another
Mocking with dance the cosmic mother
Or imitating anger in her stride.
    It fills me
      With endless pride
Ever to have known her.

    And as the days
    Peruse their ways
Across a world of endless-seeming strife
    The scavenger,
    Makes meat of her
Through thoughts of her that cut him like a knife.

Visions of an Elm Rood

I feel the vines
that are crawling round my head
and can see the ships that have sailed already
yesterday that now are passing
to and fro out there among
the apples of the sun.

And how begins the endless song
that scares away our sunset thoughts
and puts to flight the powers
of unbrightness and deceit?

What is it comes in between to petition
nature to curb her glibness?

And how could any love-song end
that asks for your forgiveness?

For the sun will say everything
    in the end.

And my heart will be listening
    when you roar.

For now, the sun only squeaks through your eyes
veiled images of columned temples
masking the warmth and glow of a self
that draws its pictures in the sand
    and from the sand
like children who are growing old
    and feel the vines
crawling round their heads.

In the Parliament of Mind

Life goes on without you.
But what is life in silence,
Trying to outshout you
In the parliament of mind?

Wine for today
Will wipe away the tears.
But what will come tomorrow
To salvage the years
That are spent in useless waiting?

And the sun cries in setting
On the other side of time
From my outmoded, manufactured
Universe of rime.

O why will not the doing
Un-entangle itself
From the abstract patterns
Of cerebral waiting?

Silently I clamor
For the shifting of gears
And the blow of Thôrr's hammer
From inside my skull

To shatter the images
Of useless bliss
That frolic in the glamour
Or pleasure of a kiss.

But life goes on
In any old way,
To please the sneering
Bishop of day

Who insists on things happening
While the years creep slowly onward
And the months and the days
And the hours and the minutes

And the seconds
And the firsts
And the nothings
And the bursts

Of negativity that swallow
The mud in which we wallow
      And throw us down
      On solid ground
To find out if we're hollow.

Prophetic Dream

I recall a queen in fairyland
      With gold upon her head.
A hundred thousand fairy lads
      Had taken her to bed.

A gentle happy queen was she
    Bathed in her regal beauty
And all of her fairy worshipers
    Were conscious of their duty.

And on a day a magus came
    In part to entertain her
But of use for wonders had she none
    And he could not detain her.

And so he worked upon her mind
    With all his skillful arts
And soon transformed her apathy
    To all that love imparts.

But the magus was an ugly brute
    Unsuited to fairy ways
And pity overtook him there
    In the finest of his days.

What misery would cover her
    If she should wake from the spell
And find a fiend embracing her
    From out of the depths of hell?

And so he touched her with his heart
    And summoned away the light
And peeled a peeling off the world
    And melted into night.

Impressions of Our First Meeting

The look of the tigress
into the eyes of the wolf
is a look of boundless
irreverence.

Hamlet is wooing
a widowed Pompadour
        in skylark land
while Denmark
is crumbling.

The sound of wolf's anger
falls on the ears of a fawn
like the clang of steel
splitting dewdrops.

True Love

Resting upon the roof and floor
of a cave deep in the earth's resounding hollow
where the howling of the night wind is still,
stalactite and stalagmite
look steadfast in each other's eyes,
longing to touch.

Lime water drips continuously
at intervals across the span of time,
like tears of longing,
poised for a while upon the brink of falling
and then released by time onto the mound
that waits below to receive its germ of growth.

And the stalagmite slowly climbs
upwards towards the encroaching king,
approaching the tender touch of his finger
across the blind millenniums of time
and a few feet of space.

And somewhere past the end
of their headlong race
they form a single pillar made of time
and stand together steadfast and sublime.

Lovesong to a Misty Veranda

Your small, purple silhouette
coming toward me in the rain,
you are umbrella to me
on the deck of my stormy ship,
you are the warm cargo in its hold.

You shelter me
where I stand scratching at the moon
as I shelter you
where you are the tickle-whisper
of the earth's loin-laughter
in my soul.

Where we walk toward each other,
water-grey pictures in the rain,
a breath is a millennium
as we breathe faster
and a century is a single footstep
as our feet scramble
on the asymptote nearer.

And we know not the rain
for we stand in the earth's hold
serene and writhing as we run
through year-less grey
without the turning of the sun
and moon and stars.

You are impatient, drenched, and cold
waiting to shield me from the torrent,
waiting for the moment
when we touch in a passioned whirlwind
of hurricane madness.

And I'm still trying to trap the instant
just before the last enfolding of ourselves together,
trying to balance it
in asymptote ever-ness.

Desert Flower

Flower that is within itself a fruitful place
yet grows upon a barren dune inside my heart,
spring up again upon this plot, that I may call
myself a forest and this heart a coffer rich
in life and beauty. Spring up again, o desert flower
molded of petals soft and fresh. Grow forth once more
and gather-in the silent mist. Spring up anew:
convey your moisture to these cracked and sun-parched lips
       that bend to sing your praise.

P.S. I Love You

    Walk, run
    Truck on by
    I'll see you on the other side

    Of the great wall
    To Neverland
    In China or in Rome

    But when willow trees
    All laugh to the song
    That weeps itself from the North Star

    I'll rest my feet
    In a puddle of ice
    And wonder where you are

Pine Song

or

After Meeting On Winsome Street

Before she has seen me
As pharaoh's chief scribbler,
      But someday she will see me as I am.

Wood that I shared my life with you
      Lest you as well might know
What it means
(,)To(e) be a messenger
      Of a peace that doesn't show.

Twenty years forgotten, twenty
Taunts 'twixt me and Oðin.
      How conceited hath she gotten,
      Cajoled the hearth-beaked raven,
While the harp-bill of the cuckoo's bird
      Quoth the sparrow nevermore.

      Witch Willow
      Was a spawow . . .

Hawk, triumphant,
      Undulates his breed
Although he seldom satiates
      The sowing of his seed.

O Saturday night,
Wert ever so far from sight
      As the blind gods have led thee!

The
Ramifications

By the 1980s, the street acid was so weak it would have taken me half a dozen hits
to even feel it, an expense I could ill afford; hence I became respectable, sort of.

The World Ahead

To figure out a grey
Wizard is hard,
Not bound by superstitions
As black wizards are.

Counterblast To Tobacco

Go back, o tobacco,
To nature, who hates your
Wasteful taste-full.

To My Mother, Remembered on Xmas Eve

On rough old turf we stand, the two of us,
each with a separate grief, his of a wife,
mine of a mother once not loved enough,
renewing constant memories of joy
evoking sorrow, constant meaning true.
Our love can only *be* true now we part,
for nothing can corrupt its fixed-in-salt
achievement of a life once lived with us,
while many through the æons stay the hope
that we remain the worthies to perceive
the light that she once shone upon our lives
from life's soft bosom and the noble heart
that pulsed within the cauldron of her art.

Solitude

The sky is empty.
For though it is full of stars,
The stars are empty.

The trees are empty.
For though they are full of life,
Life is empty.

The houses are empty.
For though they contain people,
All I see are the outer shells,
And shells are empty.

The moon is empty.
For though it is covered with rocks,
I cannot touch them.

O To Be Caught

O to be caught
        eye to eye with
            child,
See through its eyes,
        vision through them,
            feel
Something of what
        innocence makes
            real
Whisked onto the
        guardian-spirit
            wheel.

O What a Soul Won't

O what a soul won't
        do for its perceived
            other.
It will take chances,
        even, stakes are so
            high
And throw itself on
        work as its holy
            steed,
Work as opposed to
        jobs, that is, which
            only take
Time away from the
        Great Work,
Time away from the
        work that must be
            done.

Smiles on a Face I'm Fond to See

I don't know how good life can be,
     Only how good it's been today.
Smiles on a face I'm fond to see
     Have fashioned it that way.

I've never lived life to the limit
     Nor followed pleasure where it's going,
But I know even if you skim it,
     Today's was overflowing.

Night Watch

[*in my form* Trapeze]

keep watch, my spirit
do not slag
let no injunction
bend your course
relax and nature
will prevail
and turn all purpose
into rust

do not close
the eyes in sleeping
for surely dreamland
needs man's skill

even in death
take with you *there*
the things that serve you
nothing more

S o r c e r y

I wade through seas of spirits
      Upon my dismal flight,
Dim spirits of the ocean void
      That clamor for my light.

I pick among them choosing
      The ones that seem to fit
My solitary purpose here,
      These walls around my pit.

The great celestial angels
      Look down upon travail
And form instruction out of woe,
      Whose tests we mostly fail.

Yet now come I determined
      Upon this surly scene,
Resolved to make the best of things,
      Thereby my soul to wean.

There'll be no tolerating
      Of mindset or excuse
That bar my way from conquering
      The forms of fate's abuse.

For I shall walk unbowing
      Before the demon hordes
And choose the ones that seem to fit
      And harness them with words.

Feelings Upon the Loss of a Cat

I am ac-cur-sed uh-mung men;
      I am a sultry fellow.
Driven I am to drive myself
      Away from what is mellow.

Things that could soothe or lull to sleep,
    Things such as this I shun
To seek a battlefield of woe
    Yet know not what I've won.

Vain understanding have I much,
    Vain to adjust the past
From what has been: the storm is gone,
    Yet what it wrought must last.

Life is a garden of remorse
    Untended—soul transfixed
With purpose, brave yet impotent,
    Its wisdom yet unmixed.

Time can but heal the seemly hurts:
    Unseemly ones remain,
Opened and closed by what transpires
    To wake them up. The gain

Is nothing if we do not learn;
    For by its nature, guilt
Alone can neither heal the man
    Nor gather what's been spilt.

And neither does sad sorrow teach
    Without the help of joy,
Nor anything alone, even
    The things that us annoy.

Not even hours and days and years
    All filled with pain and pleasure,
Without eternity's strong hand,
    Can help one single measure.

I do not wait for anything;
    I do not count the hours
Nor expect this weed-infested field
    To spring with fragrant flowers.

For time but heals the seemly hurts;
Unseemly ones remain
Opened and closed by what transpires
To wake them up again.

Spirit Dawn

The clouds are billowing, soft white and blue
off to the east, while I my heart renew
to drag itself across another day.
Whatever rears its head to block my way
cannot, I think, much bend me from my course,
which is to plod along, like blindered horse,
not caring where the path may lead nor what
awaits me at the end of it. The rot
upon this world is only dangerous
to one who travels swiftly, while to us
who creep around unmoved it holds us up
or puts a slower poison in our cup.
The strength of twenty angels have I kept,
digits of feet and hands (these hands inept),
and armor like the mantle of the earth
surrounds me: little is can threat my worth,
          for 'tis too small to see,
          even by little me.

Whines of the aging, caterwauls of wives
whose men have bruted them, the screams of lives
wasted by statist hordes, fall short of me
and do not reach my ears. I do not see
the writing on these walls that keep me in,
these great stone Inca walls built up from sin
or sanguine spot upon the past's cold shrouds.
Even the walls themselves become but clouds
          that pass far to the east.
          I miss the swirling feast,
for I am cold as arctic grass: I grow
yet do not feel the conflicts that I know.

The Middle Pillar

Death behind me, Judgment before me,
I am the head of things: Justice.
Papess behind me, Moon before me,
I am the World, the loins: dragon-
Devil beneath me moans and bellows,
Displaced from once-usurping grace.
Upwards, the bold Magician pulls me,
Great tree that holds aloft the disk.

Elements

Earth is the teething-point:
teyt, the world-serpent.

The passive side of water
is moon, Mercury, Venus.
The active side of water
is the year and Mars.

The passive side of air
is the sun as inertial center.
The active side of air
is Jupiter and Saturn.

The 'passive' side of fire
is Urania, Queen of Heaven;
the active side of fire acts
through Uranus-Neptune-Pluto.

The passive side of the world
is the Tower of Destruction.
The active side of the world
　　　is the Lover.

A Little Help

Now when the music rises
On hillocks bold and bright,
My joy uplifts itself in triumph
And day engulfs the night.

The little spritely natures
Of things come bursting out.
In celebration of the sun,
The moon tumbles about.

Time, the impulsive hunter,
Harvests and sets his traps,
But I walk on without my feet
And fly above perhaps.

The eagle lands on certainty
But flies with the help of the wind.
And so for one who finds himself
Enamored of a friend.

Two Sonnets

O momentary vision, fluid form
that flit through lives like feather-colored birds
and ruffle feelings outward from the norm
and other things do not yet 'scribed in words,
uncanny, cunning corner of my soul
that seek me out, personified, then go
yet stay to leave a wondrous gaping hole
deep in the fabric of the things I know,
I seek you out! through æons of the pall
of past and future, sparkle that you are
amidst this massful maze or dismal wall
that stands between my senses and a star
which beckons a direction not yet gone
and seems to teach that I must carry on.

Faultless she hovers there upon my eye,
a still-fresh memory of faded bliss
reminding me that nothing is amiss
with her, only with me. I slowly die
inside while she apparently can fly
away untouched, unhampered yet by this
cold poem, poor replacement for the kiss
I'd rather hand her but the fates deny.
Her unencumbered heart I envy much,
for mine must carry all its bags alone.
She is light-hearted. I wish mine were such
that she could not have hooked it: mine is prone
to feel, be deeply moved, and by the touch
her beauty made is turning now to stone.

The Fog That Burrows Through My Thoughts

The fog that burrows through my thoughts
        Is deeper than before.
If I knew where it issued from,
        I'd wage an inner war.

Yet brightness now can penetrate,
        Potentially at least,
A greater depth of my dark life,
        Should Pan but quit the feast
And let the bold Apollo in
        To tame the sleeping beast.

Mere, Imperfect Air

What fleeting fancy love is
At times, when it is born
Aloft on wings of ecstasy
That leave the earth forlorn.

Ephemeral acquaintance,
This heaving of the heart,
Quite localized in space and time
And finished ere it start.

Great tumult and upheaval,
Great depth of wealth and joy,
Great majesty of will and thought,
Yet fragile, like a toy.

And so, what manner be it
Of thing or stance or aught
That humans may not hold it near
Nor find what they have sought?

Experience is common,
Continuing, long-lived.[*]
It saturates the wills of all
Who've wept or who have thrived.

And life has many legions
Of hours at its command,
Yet passing few are fond to taste
Or sweet, like fertile land.

Great multitude of æons,
Vast tapestry of years,
And but a moment's touch of that
Which banishes our fears.

And yet, when else can humans,
By time enslaved and trapped,
Glimpse of eternity's design
Save instants where it's tapped?

Uncounted and unmeasured
The days and hours that dawn,
Inexorably designed to dwarf
The thing that drives us on.

---

[*] rhymes with 'short-knived'

But timelessness lives *in* us
Those moments when we care
More for another's happiness
Than mere imperfect air.

The Plea of Passion

The wave arises once again,
the wave that issued from your shore.
I hope I don't make muck of it
    as I have done before.
A newly wakened spring spews forth
its clear fresh waters of intent
to wash across you, like the breeze
    that gathers up your scent.

Simmering substance welling up
from warmth, the cauldron of your eye
ensconced within your body there,
    wherein your feelings fly—
they offer chances, often missed,
to play upon your thoughts, so near
you breathe your strength into the thrust
    of what assails your ear.

Muse of a thousand faces shy
yet strong, a thousand faces bold,
smile on your poet's coy attempt
    to woo you from the cold
and wintry folds of earthen wiles
that thrive on human unconcern,
from pathways deep that mold one's thoughts
    to make a face that's stern.

Seek with clear eyes untearful, seek
with moist full lips your poet's call
and ride the tongue of fancy rooted
    upon your passage wall

and it will sing again. Unveil
the tempests of your inmost sea,
that I might canvass them and paint
  the way they look to me.

Waken to ways that mold our thoughts
to have a destination. Vague
directions end up nowhere: naught
  but purpose conquers plague,
the plague of lives that slowly fade
away and leave behind no sign
that ever other was than dust
  what once had seemed so fine.

Let go! Unhand the withered stem
and thorn. Breathe in the blossomed wind.
Let the awaited song's sad source
  caress you, like a friend.
Open your musty halls to suns
that dawn and moons that shine down in
and stars that pull away the fog
  to let the day begin.

Feasts of our high ideals, calm bliss
of worthen goals, bright pleasures round
of quests half-reached and flow'ring on,
  empowered by a sound,
these things await us, princess mine,
these depths and heights of what the mind
can see and feel and know and make
  of what the heart can find.

There are no limits, only shades
of thoughts that do not want us there.
They are as æther to my gaze
  and fluid, like the air.
My sharp eye penetrates beyond
to see the promise kept: my tongue
commands them to disperse and flee,
  obeying what is sung.

The objects of our fancies flit
like phantoms 'cross the screen of life
until the screen itself falls prey
      to sickness or to strife.
And with it goes the eye, the brain,
the heart, the flesh, the bone, the seed,
but not the self that in it dwelt
      and powered it with need.

March to the drummer deep within
who heeds no trumpet-calls of night
save as they show that when it's dark
      our thoughts can still be bright.
It's not the things we feel but that
which feels them that is sure and true.
Thus, though the body walk away,
      the I returns to you.

Anon

Ever on and ever on and on
And ever onward, ever to go on,
Ever and ever, on and on and on
Upon this path ongoing. On I tread
And on and on, on to the promised goal
Of keeping on with keeping on. I go
Onward.

Step lively!

Invocation of the Muse

This is the golden age I dreamed of,
Holding the sacred and unbowed
Close to my heart of hearts, with honor
Tapping me on the head aloud.

This is the time of waxing purpose.
This is the hour and day of need.
This is the wing that joins the other
Following eagles where they bleed.

Fashion a future worth beholding!
Vanquish the darkness of demise!
Music and writing now unfold me
Filling the space between my eyes.

Now is the path of joyous labor.
Now is the strength to will and work.
Now I become the whirling tempest
Guarding where thoughts of you might lurk.

Celebrants skip the bright fandango
Skipping it to the pure of heart
Helping to stow away libido
Priming instead the fount of art.

Follow a future worth unfolding!
Past is the darkness, made of doubt.
Here in between, the pregnant present
Lifts me aloft with song and shout.

Thus may my love be pure as roses.
Thus shall my thoughts be ample, true,
Just in event our rubbing noses
Answer my emptiness for you.

Instructions To Myself

While away the hours, but not the days—
Make them pay for every inch they take.
While away the minutes, but save the years:
Stand them upright on some platformed shelf
Away from knockings-over and upraised of earth,
The set of lessons learned. And while away the brief
Blossomings of cogentness, but do not let
Time get in the way and cause them all to pass
Either unrecorded or unscathed, for even
          Bright moments have dark insides.

Alchemy

Earth, demon of life, 'tis I the fool:
Yours is that outer realm that forced *omega*
To change to *shin* and harden into night.
But now come I to not just follow blind
And distant quests for mystery but lead
Out of the mystery that spawned deceit.

          My point?
A line of thought.
          My angle?
To eventually surface
In a solid realm.

The highest point in thought is held by knowledge,
The lowest point by earth. In between,
Lines of thought form angles of indifference
          And difference.

The Bay

Mt. Rainier over jet-red cranes
With here and there a white one
With a red tip, like a blind man's cane,
Wherever you can site one.

Seattle of my errant dreams
Announced by ferry boat-horn:
Cities are seldom what they seem,
But this one's had its moat torn

By minds of poets such as write
These little ditty dunce rimes
And seers who've regained their sight
And voices that were once minds.

To the Muse, At Twilight

Towing a barge up the straits Juan de Fuca,
    In from the ocean's seething,
Passing a freighter full-steam for the sea,
    After the trade-wind's breathing.

Over Victoria, suns have all set,
    Over the storm-waves' heaving,
And just in the moments it took to get dark,
    The tanker is gone, the barge leaving.

Comf'tablest beach on the Washington coast,
    North beach at old Port Townsend.
Hopes he in waters he gazes upon
    Loom not the ones he drowns in.

For soon he will follow his fate to the fish,
    Soon he'll the hooks be heeding,
Soon he'll be hauling in lines from the deep,
    Soon he'll the world be feeding.

But now he just leans with his face to the wind
And thinks on the her he longs for,
Thinks on the her whom he came here because,
The her that he makes his songs for.

The Dancer

Behold she is a dancer
    The dance of life she wends
Her darkling locks pursue her waist
    With myriads of ends.

The music of the moment
    Conveys its joys to her
Unhampered by the dim-lit space
    Where haughty judgments stir.

She storms the hour sweetly
    With roses on her hips
Her toes are flower petals
    Bright wreathes her parted lips.

And though her moods may vary
    They are but passing masks
The dancer dons beneath her guise
    In answer to who asks.

Her audience of one
    Is what I'll ever be
But now her restless feet have carried
    Her steps away from me
As if only beyond my transfixed
    Gaze could she be free.

Metaphor

Sadness is a woman
with wavy black hair,
with arms like willow branches
that do not catch the snow.
She casts a thick shadow
as if heavy with leaves,
and the liberties she takes
are laden with no whim of expectation.

Blinded with salt tears,
as if to clear the air
she waves her thin arms
to summon forth emptiness
and satiates her lust
with loneliness and comes
to orgasmic ecstasy
only in death.

Three Songs to the Waning Moon

1. The Leaning Buffalo

A vision approaches,
not the one I seek
but a small vision,
a side vision.

For a moment,
my feathers fly:
I raise my lance,
charging the iron buffalo.

But then I am the rail,
a single rail, unpaired—
off into the distance I go,
one rail, alone.

And the iron bison leans
to one side and falls,
and the single rail goes on
beyond the hills of rain

to the dream time,
to never was
and ever was
and wasn't . . .

to the dream time,
the ever was
that never was,
or was it?

I am the rail
that rides itself,
for the iron bison
rides it not.

For it needs two
to ride up on,
and I am one,
alone.

2. Two Old Bones

The old man walks
silently to the tops of hills
and peers over
into the valley of the Wasichu[*] dread.

That which lies
on the other side of all hills
is the valley of the smoke holes
    that have no tipis.

And an old man peers back,

---

[*] Lakota term for those who brought forged iron and lies

that same old man, back
from the valley of the smoke holes
    that have no tipis.

Between them, they make a youth,
    the two old men.
Between them, they make a man,
    the two old bones.

3. Rattle

Rattle my heart, o wayward wind
    of anger.
Rattle my bones, yon wayward noises
    of the stone-hut men.
Rattle my world,
    thought-crushers,
        ringing wires.
Rattle my skull,
    for skulls do make the world.

Rattle, viper:
be like the big
brother, fanged
    and stiff-tailed.

Rattle, wind,
rattle on,
for no-one's listening save I,
    and I am nothing.

After the Distant Sleep

Do I feel the bones of my psyche
Stirring after the distant sleep
Of enterprises that bore no fruit
    And love that bore no laughter,
    Love that bore no laughter?

Can the wind-borne sylphs of the forest
Bear my song to the highest trees
Though it has sprung from deep, deep wells
    Whose origin is darkness,
    Thoughts conceived in darkness?

Paint my image, o shades of wanting,
Paint so fortune may mend its path:
Hem the limitless light with shape
    That life might follow after
    And life might follow after.

Dark Mood of Yesterday

Fly away, fly away,
Dark mood of yesterday.
You are no-longer welcome here.
This is no place for you to stay.

For my ungraceful heart is full
And I can only strive to pull
My life from underneath the wool:
    We've passed your part of the play.

You serve no purpose anyhow.
Where once you heralded the truth,
The truth of life is different now.
You're but a vestige of my youth
That once resided on my brow
And made my attitudes uncouth,
    But not anymore, I pray.

For while your back was turned on me
I healed my wounds and set you free
To prey on someone else's glee
    Like an unwanted stray.

Workshop
'Gems'

To Brighid
[*who doesn't object to adverbs and gerunds*]

sedately succumbing
the dizzyingly dismal dawn
had a brightly brazening
awakening

switching to lively
a deftly beckoning
tree-top-like bobbing-about
is happening

intriguing how airily
spritely it's becoming
it's just slightly numbing
but merrily

The Importance of Tea

before *t* is an *at*
after it a *ta-ta*
        rat-a-tat-tat

it all hinges on whether the *n*
is before the *t* or after it
before it it's a *note*
        the information
after it a *tone*
        the spin

mate   tame
innate   tiny
late   tail
        (spin)
nips
        (*spin*)

and an eaten dna

before *t* is an *at*
after it a *ta-ta*
        rat-a-tat-tat

Night at Nikkis (Venice Beach)

The pulse can't feel me
nor I the pulse
except in snippets
but this is good

It could get contentious
if we locked sonnets
like horns
on stone causeways

They are bright at night
lit like sets
this carousel
a waking dream

It runs in rivulets
down the side
of the sound of the tide
draped like droplets

Take me to your intelligentsia
I'll pick their pockets

a poem should end at the redundant rime

so
you've set yourself up down here
where coming round to a proper finish
has been a prolonged haunted longing's
wish
eh

well
the lay of the language is
that it languishes
like a fish in too small
a bowl
whose wall of tall plastic
's too thick for the fish
to get
even
the least bit pricklish
about where it might get a fair bout
ere it go out with a flourish

fight! man or woman
(for bards are both)
yes it is iffish

unless you know where fate's ticklish
and've already made your wavering wish-list
and kissed it bye-bye in triplicate

for it was 'to go'
and you're a goldfish

Instructions with Regard to Hair

if it's tall
has hair (preferably dark)
and is pleasant to look at
    marry it

if it's of medium height
has hair (preferably light)
and is pleasant to look at
    hunt with it

if it's short
has hair (preferably soft)
and is pleasant to look at
    pet it

if it's small
hairy
and black
    step on it

if it's small
hairy
and green
    smoke it

Diptych

VERTICAL

Which of the four
real directions—
up, out, down, or in—
are eyes drawn
by a pearl's glow
or gutters about a roof's rim?

What cry echoes off
the dunes' soft drifts
to prickle with the cacti
at dawn's injunction?

Incense of lizards
amidst moist
ferns has *what*
to say to me
not already whispered to others?

Was it the hope I would not hear?

Ten fiddles while skateboards' click-scrape-click
      way to the end of the world
      where it all goes on

HORIZONTAL

copper mists this turquoise face
malachite effervesces
flora from giants' lips drips onto
      sand made flesh
      word made sand

onto the graded must the concrete flow
to avoid frontage ditches and dry
scrub even serpents shun
      (mine went before)

<pre>
beyond
        only
the thorned beasts
and horned ghosts
        go
somnambulantly imitating
        the young of stucco
</pre>

The Poet Laments His Deviated Septum

<pre>
It feels as if
the lack of rain
is my doing.
It feels as if
I'm holding back
the solar flare
that would wipe clean
the earth's surface
for renewing,
that would wipe clean
the mind of man
with a fanfare.

I am not numbed
yet cannot weep
and breathe. Witness:
an eye not numbed
would better weep,
unloading time.
But I don't feel
loneliness, I
am loneliness.
I dare not weep
and only cry
in pantomime.
</pre>

Recent
Stuff

(from about the turn of the century on)

What WAS He Doing!

There was once a strong wind, and it blew me
where I'd not meant to go, and this threw me
     for a loop, till I managed
     to recover undamaged
all my clothes, for the people there knew me.

Elephant Bones

in a remote graveyard
     of big bone
     and curving tooth
the often gentle giant danced
his slow dance, weaving
mourning into motion side to side
holding what was once rooted
     in a friend
     or in some kin
     long
lost to time
     though not to memory

upraised, this day
a day of dance
whose dance is death
     simpering
     silent

the camera caught it in its frame
     like the trapped bird
     it was

the camera captured it for me
     that I might watch
     mournful

For My Father

And so dawns the second full
day without my dad. Life
lumbers loudly on, day's
step by day's awkward step.
Who can fathom why it keeps on
lumbering along. Time's
ear for poetry is gone,

only its eye remains, softly
seeing what I do each day
with scant remark. *I* have not fallen,
and yet I am laid low. Hope
has fallen. Joy has fallen. Time,
the creep, creeps on, and I with it,
armed to the teeth for war with God.
I train by reaching for the sky
to pull it down. "March . . . forth,"
he said to me. Though lacking tongue
to say it with, he chose the day
to say, "March fourth, I went away."

That Great Whore Babylon

child of the great river
city of marvels
luxuriant growth mocking the have-nots
        in their barrenness
as it spills from terraces
like the boughs of the willows whereon we hang our harps
        to hear the wind weeping

what business
might the gods have in preserving opulence
save for feeding sacrifice
        and divine appetites

child of the great river
city of marvels
luxuriant growth that mocks the have-nots
        in their barrenness

Brief Lecture on Correct Pronunciation of *Short-Lived* and *Niche*
[*Interlocking Limericks*]

There once was a poet whose stint
making use of the fruits of the mint
    was as fleet and short-lived
    as his anger short-knived—
you would think that he might take a hint.

But the stubbornness in him connived
with the artistry on which he thrived
    to compel he insist
    by the Muse he be kissed,
whence the poverty in him derived.

As a poet, he knew that his fist
was his tongue when it came to the list
    of the people whose acts
    were indictable facts
and who had all the things that he'd missed.

Now of honor life's turmoil exacts
but a single thing: never be lax
    and expect in reward
    what a dragon might horde
(what Raskolnikov got with an axe).

Such a treasure might yield to the sword,
but then afterwards where's the accord:
    you may revel in bitches
    and volumes of riches
but who died and made *you* a lord?

Though living has left him in stitches,
he accepts it all, even the glitches,
    as exactly the tint
    it's to be, by Luck's dint—
even poets can relish their niches.

Transformed by the Undergrowth

<pre>
        another day
        another dawn
another dusk of a day gone
        and not a lot
        to show for what
the psyche's been up to

there seem to be myriads
of little time periods
that make up each lifetime
        we cut to

then suddenly one of 'em
        will come of it
        and summon in
another type of dawn
        for determining
        the where and when
of everything that's wrong
        that we can mend

it seems as if
it all works out
        in the end
</pre>

Land of the Fays

<pre>
atop this bald plateau
        eyes acquiesce
to take in greening folds
        through which moments
unwrap themselves in glens
        scaring shadows
away from thought's prime brush
        with beauty's bark
</pre>

outweigh my heart with beats
      of light's rhythm
where birdsong bays at moons
      its wisdom sees
in the sky's far facets
      these sparkling wells
our eyes the skinless gem's
      hazy setting

bold dew and gentle rain
      compete with breath
for space between curtains
      of furry plays
where understanding loafs
      half serious
tinged with mysterious
      ungentled ways

no need for toning down
      must vault these wards
of angel temperaments
      the healing rows
whose shades waver from straight
      more than a bit
and find unfractal form
      in the soft breeze

no machine-made moments
      are hoarded here
in deference to trolls'
      waking scowling
sleep in the dimmed harp strokes
      where fluttered leaves
ponder us a journey
      that makes no waves

The Mad Seer-Poet

What price greatness
in verse's realm
holding forth at song's prow
but not its helm

The treasured Muse
steers for far shores
us who brave the long haul
all without oars

Wind's vagaries
determine pace
while inspiration guides
with poker face

I put my trust
in the long haul
while storm's sharp happenstance
distracts the thrall

Waiting to Give Birth Till All the Actors Were Present

The star on the top of the tree
Is to honor the one by which 'three'
    Of the Wise Men were drawn
    To the Lord's side to fawn
While he yet was a tyke on one's knee.

As convinced as some are the Nativity
Had Three Wise Men near the vicinity,
    Should we sculpt the *wee babe*
    Nearly *two years* of age?
For a virgin birth, quite a delivery!

The Terror of the Ants Speaks

I am the terror of the ants:
I tower high above them.
Where any cross my casual glance,
they learn I do not love them.

For I, with oft bit fingers, mash them
each to a bloody glob
and flick or toss or, blowing, stash them
in trash cans by the mob.

I relish each entailed demise
of tickly creature crawling
where I do not allow, my eyes'
domain their plain of mauling.

But just what is it now that looms
above *my* path, its shade
darkening days with thoughts of tombs
whose walls I would evade?

Dalet, a Jib on the Sea's Swells

a song wells while the swinging sail
exerts translation's needs astride
the sea's swells while I grip the rail
to burrow through this stormy tide
that drives tongues as its whips assail
these rearing equine waves I ride

intense screeching of startled birds
decries the pulsing vessel's pace
as cross-questioning's nimble words
confront deceptive power's place
where numb nabobs attend the herds
we were before we braved this race

the winds' freedom empowers thought
beyond the confines of the maze
which past masters of hearing wrought
to keep their minions in a daze
of calm heedless of what they sought
ere ease had robbed them of their ways

so stand stalwart with chin unbowed
and face the ocean's mighty press
unfazed rather than join the crowd
whose verses wreak of listlessness
while mind's liveliness cries aloud
to break all landward chains of stress

The Human

it was an attempt to be
a dissimilitude
that prompted me to come over here and almost grasp
your hand in an obsequious way

is it me or are your mental shirttails hanging out
and I'm looking at myself when I say this
are we for real?

often echoes of sandbagged thoughts come drifting by
      and dribble about
        with the boisterousness
      of someone else

spooled seas throb beneath
to the weight of moon and sixpence of its paltry thoughts
past-packer and stuck-with stew
true to the crimson wood that it once knew

I Am Russian Wolfhound

I am Russian wolfhound.
Master is German author.
I do not understand what he writes.
He writes in German.
I am fluent only in Russian and English.
My master is foolish, otherwise
he would have someone translate into
language somebody would actually read.

Am picking up rudimentary German.
Have to in order to pretend to obey him.
(*I am only following orders.*)
If he ask me to do something
beneath my dignity or immoral
I bark (in Russian) and say I cannot.
He would not dare spank me.
(I am too big.)

There are other dogs in neighborhood.
They are not Russian wolfhounds.
Some are size of lunch
(but I don't eat them).
I growl at the German shepherds.
This makes my master livid
(he takes it as ethnic slur).

Some days are very good.
These are days when my master's young relatives
visit and play game where I knock them over
then they ride me.
It is fun.
They have fun.
I have fun.
My master likes me on such days
more than usual (he gives me treats).

Not all Germans are bad.
My master is well-meaning.

He lacks proper teeth
for anyone to be afraid of him.
Some people are afraid of me.
Dogs, however,
seldom are,
even if they are size of lunch
(since they do not have concept of lunch
like I do).

I intend to continue to be moderately happy
manipulating my master into better behavior
than he would otherwise display.

I am Russian wolfhound.

Drinking Song in the Style of the Goliards

Think you I can't drink you down
    underneath yon table?
You, my friend, start out a clown,
    I both quick and able.
While your brain gets bogged and bent,
all your limbs (and member) spent,
    I, a poet, wander
    past the fumes you squander.

Spirits of the brewer's art
    saturate the shallow,
whereas it is just the start
    for a mind that's fallow
soil no more but seeded through
with this lesson just for you,
    jocular in meter
    (laughing at your peter).

In an age of masks, I remember faces

better than names, but not so well
as I should like, were I astute
and could contest, without much pause
from reticence, the leadership
of the vacuum, but nothing soars
on wings of gold, whose leaden sheen
will pull one down, or sideways. Flesh,
be satisfied, within your cage
of wizardry, to taste of lore
and aftermath, as unprepared
as ever faith, distressed by shoals
or lack of wealth, might tend to see
its tendency, however fierce
the face once felt, in times of endless
endearing strife, whose call to arms
seems squalid now, considering
that ends desired, precluded since
from lack of taste, await the age
of once again, and not this buzz
of new bazaars, whose products add
to night's divide, undisciplined
by freedom's wail
     of a madness
misunderstood
     by the faceless

Tanist

Not far enough to compass half my world,
The half that's in her eyes.

Obscure at best was where I stopped and you began.
Your being drank my being, flowing since
Confined within your greater bed
Whose ocean is the stars.

Yesterday

Yesterday, I saw your living room
through the front window while I 'taxied' by
that place where once we played while Carl Orff played
his Carmina Burana on us
lit from the window through the courtyard
dimly lit in late afternoon

A head was silhouetted toward me
for me it was your head
and there was I beside you tongue in cheek
(my tongue in your cheek)

And with you I was in the master bedroom
      when your folks arrived
      and we were caught
      and I was banished
and then with you again the morrow
at dinner while your pop made peace
based on your assurances
that I had been a gentleman
      and true.

And eye beside you by the backyard pool
      on sunny summer afternoons
whiling with you the hours I was paid for
      to not go back too soon and give
      the regular mailman a bad name.

Those were days with thunder-clouds approaching
seeking to strangle-off my world from you
that summer when our hearts were basking
within each other's warmth and smooth caress
      a comforting stillness
not knowing what we sensed that was to come

Love Alone

Love has its own momentum:
It is its own reward.
Even without its object fair,
It is, of life, the lord.

It cannot fly on one wing:
It needs must fly on two.
Yet having flown, it then sustains
Itself on thoughts of you,
      On thoughts of you.

The Secret of the Trees

Even if you were spoken for,
I'd not know how to love another
while you yet whisper on this woodland sphere.

Charmed by my guarded memory of you
(untouched for twenty years and more)
I steep myself in yore, to break the bit,
snap the fence, in hopes 'twill cure the fit
of pure stupidity that drove me hither
      into this blind corral.

Was it not you that told me once
that I should tackle life more humorously?
Well I insist on taking it *both* ways,
both humorously and sourly in my sore and wondrous need.

My Medicine Staff

Life becomes sweeter by the hour. I gather
up my trail of toil into
medicine bags of wonder. My staff
consists of three Christmas trees
coiled together, entwined with eels.

In it, I concentrate my power,
etched effortless onto a world
still mindful. It teaches
my inner senses each time my eyes
savor it sideways and sigh.

And in this charm, bound up, is life
supporting love. And in this charm,
set free, is love, supporting life.
Each supports each! and other things
that fit in the nooks and crannies.

Welcome Clouds

Life is a melancholy joy,
A sorrowful delight
Imbued with darknesses and clouds
That triumph over night.

Conclusion to "He Grew To Stop Them"

A sorrow to himself he will remain
while cheering up the songbirds and the hens
who lay the eggs he laughs at. Aimless tears
meander down his face into the beard
he grew to stop them.

A Case of All Dressed Up

All my life, I've been a case of
"All dressed up, no place to go,"
Like I was grown for something better,
Like I was groomed to bite the wind
      And then no wind arose.

Summon the day, with all its longings!
Summon the seasons of the drifts!
Summon the dawn, with its soft partings
Sundering him who's not too swift,
      In whom no wind arose.

Chiasmus

If one night is this hard
without her, how will I last a year?
And if a year, what then? Surely pain
that cannot last forever cannot last
the night, and yet I sense no end to it.

And I have naught to blame except my folly
that led me to embrace a world of things
and leave behind that thing which was the world
to me. If suffering exists to teach,
then I have learned. And if what's empty gapes
in order to be filled, then I am full
of emptiness, like eyes that gather wool.

To the Calm

Fortune smiles
on those with restraint
on such as yourself
my fair Diana
and that is why I love you
like a storm making love
to the calm.

Song: Untitled

Why do the streams that wash the silt away describe my course
Why can't the winds that blow my love to me become my horse

Why did I never learn to ride
Why did I only learn to hide
From what I really feel inside

There is an ancient tale that's told about an anguished heart
That finds its love fulfilled but only after years apart

Why can't the years be kind to me
My love is endless like the sea
For she is everything to me

The ancient arts of necromancy can do me no good
What I would raise was never dead, only misunderstood

And now I hear its anguished cry
Chained and held, it wants to fly
And give homage to the sky
And give homage to the sky

Love's Fool

However, o ye gods,
you choose to make me happy,
do not at the expense
of my love. Her pleasure
is that on which *I* feast;
and if any upset it,
on them will I wreak havoc,
be assured. Though I am not
trained in man's warfare,
warfare with the gods
I know. So do not make
fools out of all of us
by testing the resolve
of one who is a fool
but for love.

Patterns In the Wind

The world builds its monuments
To Adam and its monuments
     To Eve.
The world builds its monuments
But I like not monuments
     That leave

A sour taste in mouth or a
Sourness of spirit
     In a friend
So I build no monuments
But only leave patterns
     In the wind.

A Dangerous Charm

Tethers, feathers, fate that weathers,
Feel our fortune's kindness bloom:
Conjure winter's secret hinters,
Shivers of an eerie room.
Blossom, possum, rule and boss 'em:
By the power of Nightmare's groom,
Pluck the heartstrings like they're smart-strings,
Please the demons to their doom.

She has a dangerous charm,
a dangerous charm about her
that many have wondered at,
I'm sure, and I'm one.

She has a dangerous charm,
a dangerous charm about her
that could persuade the hillocks
to move if she'd a mind to.

She has a dangerous charm,
a dangerous charm about her
about eight lines long which
I'm giving to her now.

She has a dangerous charm, yes,
a dangerous charm about her
that I seek to dispel
with my soul-searching laughter.

Flower of the Mind

I bring my love a flower of the mind
instead of flowers of a different kind
requiring water, care, and explanation
of where she got them from: her consternation
is not my cup of tea. And yes, she knows

this flower in my mind is one that grows
only for her: the water of my tears
sustains its growth, and does so in arrears.
It seems to me that such a blossom's hue
is only ever seen by wondrous few.
It seems to me that such a blossom's scent
might prove to be a thing of wonderment
so rare even the seed producing it
      might cause a reasoning man
      to brave the fiery pit.

Fruit of the Tree Hunger

I steel myself for the long haul,
      disposed to keep the faith.
Over the barren, seedless wastes
      I hover, like a wraith.

Who once had known sweet serpentine
      delights and soft embraces
Now needs must shed his skin to fit
      the narrow, rocky places.

This inhospitable terrain
      is not exactly new.
It looks exactly like the crags
      he's grown accustomed to.

Yet now he knows another place
      one that is moist and green
One that's forbidden to his gaze
      and must remain unseen.

But the mind's eye will not go shut:
      it tempts the heart with sights
Of lands rich and bowed with fruits
      that offer tempting bites.

And so in turmoil now he waits
    preparing for the fast.
He needs must round temptation steer
    to hunger's lair at last:

Hunger, the end of all his searching
    hunger, the final prize
Hunger, the tree that bears the fruit
    that makes the foolish wise.

Song of Meditation

The world centered upon this spot
    Is my domain.
If any are to rule it,
    It must be me.
You rule your own world, other being,
    For back is towards oneself
And all things return to their creator.

The three circles around this place
    Describe a sphere
But remain circles nonetheless.

One revolves around my backbone
    Like dances
One around my line of sight
    Like clocks
And one around the stick across my lap
    Like a horse mating
    Or horses rearing.
It is this last I walk around
Whenever I walk in a sacred manner:
All walking is sacred
And so should be its manner.

Spirit of the six directions,
Lead me in but one, but make it a good one.

Show me the gift that I can give
     To my poorer tribesmen
And also to the ones that are rich
     But poor in spirit.
Show me the gift that I can give myself
For I am the recipient of all my actions
And must hear every word that I speak.

Spirit of the six directions,
Teach me to walk in a sacred manner.
Prepare me to walk the seven steps
That reach the hub of life's great wheel
That wise axle that stays forever
     Motionless and moving.

Spirit of the six directions,
Sky-father, earth-mother,
Thunder beings of the west,
White giant of the north,
Star-herald of the east,
I am in the south: find me!

The Riddle of the Sphinx

Experience of life,
     Through which I walk alone,
Has danced before my eyes,
     Repeated, like the drone
Of something softly spoken
     Which thunder cannot hear,
Alone within its musings,
     Accounted far or near.

Be hush! my lady comes:
     Her footfalls pierce the night
With echoes of hereafter
     And that wherein I might
Should time perceive us walking

Together in the wood
With arm in arm there laughing
          But linger where she stood.

The distant, pompous rumblings
          Of mortal dragons wheeze.
Their queen, the moon-god's sister,
          Relaxes at her ease.
"I hear you not, yon hell-hounds
          That chase the serpent's tail!
My spirit waxes newly made
          And leaves an empty trail."

The clock is fiercely ticking,
          And yet my ears hear naught.
A furrowed brow besets my head:
          My servant is distraught.
"What ails you, regal master,
          What ill, that you so brood?
The night bespeaks your temper
          With noises rash and rude!"

"What sounds? I cannot hear them
          That trickle noiselessly
Beyond the veil of tempests
          Which rage yet cannot be."
"What is it that arouses
          These tempests that you speak of?
They must be great to silence
          These sounds the heavens reek of!"

"One force, none other, stirs them,
          Awakens them to broil
And leads them to envision
          A goal that will not spoil.
My dream sense has awakened
          With visions clear as day
Yet cannot hear her footsteps
          With thunder in the way.

"A terrible, swift purpose
    Has settled on my brow
And sends my head a-reeling
    Beyond the here and now.
My sight in me is stirring—
    I see it clear as dawn!
And yet, I cannot grasp it
    Where time goes blindly on."

What lover rides inside us,
    Unnoticed by the eye,
Who seeks only to cushion
    The place wherein we lie?
What lover hides within us,
    Unmanifest to all,
Who seeks but to unravel
    The distance that we fall?

Where night becomes the tempest,
    Becoming is its calm,
Which follows ever after
    To make a healing balm.
And relishing the darkness
    Wherein the Light would shine,
It knows itself in silence:
    The double, squared, of nine.

At Morn

At morn, the sky donned its headdress,
its layers of beautiful cloud-beings
of myriad variety and number,
from fluffy white to indigo,
small to large, plain to intricate:
the sky gave the sky depth,
a depth of spirit to feed the eye
and brain-stuff of him who observes,
    but nothing for the heart.

A painter would have to be swift as a horse
to capture the spirit of each passing feather
donned by day and soon torn off
by the sun's torch, that noble headdress
and all its feathers lost to the wind:
a battle lost, the sky-god slain,
the heat and stillness settling upon us,
     and nothing for the heart.

Music

Waves of a music sad or light
No longer catch me wallowing
But flow right through me, sideways
Or front to back, following

The good red road through me,
Where I'm a window to the sky
And shine with white, fluffy clouds
Or pulse with dull, grey ones. I

Have followed chord and melody
Deeper within me than an ocean
To where they lead, onward,
Seeking the bright and glowing notion

That sometimes, somber, from within
Or from the air outside me
Molds from the focuses of moments
Great purposes that guide me.

Music, your moods beat down against
My sympathetic drumhead,
Now that I've felt those moods myself
And am no more a numb-head.

Voice That Inspires Me

She reverberates like the soft
gurgle-ing of a brook
only continuous-sounding,
continuously pulsing
like a motor revved-up sort-of
no-place-to-drag-race-type-
sound, as I recall it
just now as I heard it,
its soft purr excluded
by the vast, awful distance
her cheek is from the breath
inspired in me by her
and how far her neck is
from my hand.

Awaken me, o siren
of no bad emergency,
you who have awakened me
before.

For the Light flows into
your head and then out of
your mouth and then into
my me! o bearer
of brightness.

O light-bearer,
light wearer
upon my tolerance,
on my impatience,
like Lucifer, you have fallen
within my estimation
from the abstract to the concrete,
outside to in.
So speak fluid motions
into the scheme of things,
o breather of humors
that I do not.

Speak fluid harmony
into me, not
a dissonant tune.
Yet speak to me truthfully,
do not paint sunshine
the moon.

Distances Within

Distant vision of my soul,
Vision of what my soul might be
Given a year or two or three . . .

Vision, distant, of my soul,
Don't go away, but stay with me,
Stay to become the thing I see . . .

Vision of my distant soul,
    Make nearer, nearest,
    Hearer, here
The changes as they now appear
    In the distances within me,
    In the distances within.

The Shrinking Race of Men

Earth is the dried blood of giants.
The skull of Ymir is the sky.
These things are well known:
What's not understood is why.

Men chase their phantoms
And phantoms chase their tails
But only the men wonder
Why all their chasing fails.

Phantoms have no knowledge
Nor capacity for same.
Yet all men who lack it
Will feel it in their shame.

And so some may seek it
And some from it may hide,
Both thinking beyond themselves
Instead of deep inside.

It happens that there's more
To a man than meets the eye
And more to life than what transpires
'Twixt birth and when you die.

Yet that is not what's taught us
In the desert of our schools
So is it any wonder
The world's made up of fools?

Earth is the dried blood of men—
A shrinking race are we,
For what's inside us all runs out
To mingle with the sea.

Desiring What Cannot Be Attained

You who fathom into me
      With eyes that seek, that quest,
I see your face turned up at me,
      Am drawn to seek the rest.

It follows from the soft brown eyes
      And soft yet bony face
That turns my way, somewhere beneath
      Awaits a softer place.

I seek the haven from all want,
    The fuel of all desire,
Which even speaking of consumes
    My frame within its fire.

And yet it finds no avenue
    Except in memory,
And so the flame recoils unspent
    Into the heart of me.

To Songs of Others

How sweet the purple images
Spun by the poets pastoral
    That passed before.
How fortunate that they could carve
Such lofty images in time
    To still be heard.
How nice for them they learned to paint
Colorful pictures for the ears
    Of soft-skinned maidens.
My images are carved of steel
By light of street lamps and recited
    To songs of others.

What undeniable surcease
Of squalor sits on ancient lines
    That pages graced.
What catacombs of figured speech
Surround the lofty themes of old
    Like temple grounds.
My verses eat the seeds of crows
And sing of how my garden grows
    On coffee grounds.

What Merely Looks Sublime

You should have seen the clouds this morning,
Gathered in their council sky:
The separate tufts of grey and purple,
Thousands strewn about. And I,

Who longed to be among them, floating,
Blended with the lords of rain
The winds had brushed together, managed
No such life aloft to gain.

The visual enchantment woven
Over all who faced this morn
Enchanted *me* the most, I'll wager.
Yet, because this flesh is torn

By feelings finding no fruition
In what's near of place and time,
My mind's moved the least, I'll wager,
By what merely looks sublime.

Beyond the Bounds
or
Rhyme Run Amuck

When she is harsh, I weep she loves me not.
And when she's sweet, I weep for I am hot
To have her though I know our souls would rot
In hellfire should we give our love a shot
(Assuming we were each within arm's plot).
It's true I'd brave vile ills to find out what
Precisely it required to stir her pot
Of potions (make her frenzied, hot to trot),
Yet on this plan what puts a major blot
Is that such ills, which slow *me* not one jot,
Would fall on *her* as well; and so my cot
Remains the abode of one: the gaping slot

Beside me waxes empty, like some lot
That has no building on it, just a yacht
Reminding us of some exotic spot
That's far beyond the bounds of what we've got.

The Horse Culture

O Great Spirit of earth and sky,
Earth, our mother, and sky, whose seed
Begets us, why did you raise me up
To love your people, the horse culture,
And yet denied me the good battles,
The good hunts, a good lodge?
Was it to feel lament and sorrow?
There is enough of that already
To fill the oceans. Was it to teach
How fleeting be the things we value
Most? Yet all is fleeting: why
Was this peculiar heart's desire
Chosen to illustrate that fact?

O Great Spirit, my lodge is round
Like that of chiefs, for it's the world
That houses me. It's love I hunt,
With Cupid's darts, and battles have I
Galore: I need but think on those
Whose faults presume to govern us
And I have wars enough to last
My heart till all its blood runs out
       And memories subside,
Old memories of earthly splendor
       And tents of aurochs hide.

Storm Over Year's End

Nothing but dull dankness
      Partaking of my bones.
Normally, grey weather
      Is cheerful to my soul.
Dismal, the vast sky-sponge
      Is squeezed into our eyes.
Child of the Great Mother
      Must play indoors awhile.

Note how confined torment
      Is softened and spread out:
Can it embrace lifetimes
      Within its air-tight shroud?
Note how the bright playful
      Transmutes to dull surcease,
Deafened by elf-drumming
      Which on the pavement beats.

Hovering proud vulture
      Whose wings have hugged the ground,
Boundless, the soft storm-cloud
      With fringes dripping down
Captures the whole moment
      As seen from where I'm perched,
Coaxing the green richness
      Of eucalyptus earth.

Dapples of lit silver
      Have cracked right through the lead,
Herding the massed darkness,
      As if it would compress
All into one bosom,
      That bosom being mine,
All into one bosom
      That is not judged sublime.

Still, in the end darkness
      Prevails upon the wind,

Heralding chill evening,
    Whose emptiness we live.
Swallowed, the bold skylight
    On which brave dreams have fed
Closed with a sly flourish
    Its stubborn dome of lead.

Conclusion to "Time Will Know"

You leave me only words for friends:
They use me for their timeless ends,
Bending the fabric of my woe
To mold the verse that time will know.

Eyes
[*Pseudo-Petrarchan*]

Eyes . . . looking at me unwavering
a mere two inches distant, eyes whose gaze,
devoid of guile, cuts through the surface maze
to reach my very center, a sobering,
uplifting thing those eyes, whose coloring
has haunted me since first they aimed their rays
upon my person: eyes which force obeys
as if of my dominion they were king.
When my eyes rest on them, drink hers as deep
my azure rings as mine do hers the hue
of moist, rich earth? Our fondness seems to seep
by slow osmosis along our beams of sight,
as if each waiting breast they would imbue
with tincture of it to withstand the night.

A Throne to Her

Her spunk is mythical!
Her humor laughable,
Her skin so touchable,
     How can I stay my hand!
Her glow a-burgeoning
Amid the drizzle-ing
Evokes a hankering
     To rise to her command.

Convey a throne to her,
O lofty conifer,
For she's the ravisher
     That plucks my pagan soul
And lifts its infancy
Beyond the canopy
Of strife and infamy
     To play its purposed role.

Did Not Give a Name

You are my desert spring. You are
My reasons for pressing on: my jewel
Of purpose and my train of thought.
You are the light I wish I'd known
Awaited me when darkness triumphed
In me and stole away my youth.
You are better than a good book,
You who have no end, and now
My own plot is a mystery.
Life is a glorious, if painful
Lesson in what I'm looking for
     But did not give a name,
No,
     Did not give a name.

Beneficent Spell

Furrows within the mind, I've plowed them.
Seeds of our golden thoughts, I've sown them.
Now I await the sun to call them
    Forth from the rocky earth.

Paths to the high plateau, I walk them.
Taverns along the way, I pass them.
Sights that would lure the eye, I mock them,
    Seeking a truer worth.

Tables piled high with meats, they gorge them!
Fleshly delights, they cannot shun them,
Know not the way to choose among them,
    Strengthened by ancient mirth.

I am the fool who will amuse them.
I am the magus that will rule them.
I am the world and still confuse them,
    Changing with each rebirth.

Rejuvenating Wind

Like a cool breeze on a hot summer's day,
You blow into my nooks and crannies
And aërate my soul.

You strike my cobwebs off with brooms
And make a habitable place
Again out of my cellars.

And the monsters that eat at me
Are finding me too tough now,
Although I find me tender.

Come and do it all again!
Musk-melon, honeydew,

Seedless watermelon . . .

Come and do it all to me
Over and over and over again
And over again some more.

Unifying Concept:
Tribute to Chief Dan George
[*think of it as in his voice*]

The wind blows
    The same direction
    The ground is going.
It's the *prevailing* wind,
    Of course, that I'm speaking of.
The wind blows
    The same direction
    The ground is going.
Perhaps this
    Is telling us something.
    Do you think?

The wind blows
    The same direction
    The ground is going
And that direction
    Is where the sun
    Always comes from.
Perhaps these things
    Are telling us something.
    Do you think?

The Conqueror Worm

The leaves of the trees
        that are turning auburn
and yellow-gold
        and garrulous scarlet
have become drab
        to my delving eye.
There's no great riddle:
        night is the hunter,
not day. Who deems
        darkness sovereign
sees straight the stark beyond,
        where staid dusk conquers.

Light of the Moon
[*Pseudo-Petrarchan*]

Light of the moon, fair object of the sun,
purpose of breezes in the midst of heat,
brave force of love, reason that fruit is sweet
and nuts nourishing, origin of fun,
light that escapes its chains when work gets done,
that which is bound to light when we compete,
that which comes nearest making life complete
upon this agèd rock—amazing one,
I wouldn't want to contemplate what life
might likely have been like had I not found you,
or what it's like for those who do not know you.
I know what life is like when not around you:
the other planets spin around below you
and stir the æther with their waves of strife.

Zenryu

yesterday was the equinox
last night I dreamt I got the letter
you never mailed

Singing to the Trees

Whom shall I call
      To hear the plaintiveness
Of my wail?

The caterwauling of saints
      Will attract a crowd,
But I am an acquired taste.

And who shall listen?
      Not just hear
But listen?

I was conceived
      For one purpose
(Besides the world's)
And that was
      To sing sweetly
In Beauty's ear
Across pages
      Of crushed trees
And wishes, one
Who *can* listen
      And comprehend
The thing I sing.

But when she listens not
      It is then that I must
Soldier on
      Singing
To the trees.

And Brave Diana

Whenever some quirk of fate renews the song
Of *freedom* in these unsoldierly veins of mine—
Though time may not again bless us with such
For many decades, even centuries hence,
We being dullards now—when memory
Of Scottish ages passed by Braveheart calls
These arteries of poetries to war
And glorious rebirth: when eagles call
'Midst sparrows—when the feeling of the breeze
Overcomes all the swamplands of the lee
That lie within me, then is when I rise
To purpose, raise myself up from my bones
And chant within my mind the fiery chant
That sells me on its object from the start
And raises hackles here, that I not sleep
But persevere to be this incarnation
And fierce expression, while these lungs yet pump,
Of Love's freedom to love, even over
Objections righteous from my point of view
And yours as to the rightness of that love
Right now or as to whether it was right
When it was . . . and in the innocence of life's
Necessary consequence of what it strives
To be that is not driven by the wind
Of hurricanes—nor even supernovae—
But only by that breeze that once on me
Poured forth from inside lips that once poured forth
On me their softness and their sanctity
That made me, even though a sore sinner,
At least a sinner who's sinned on distant clefts
Of distant cliffs of ridges distant yet
From where I was when birth was new and I
Still ignorant and afraid. For should I die
A death not half so hideous and grand
As Wallace's, I still had lived a life
And loved a love as few have loved or lived
Since I was born the hundredth time ago
If I was born at all. And had she known,

Mother of mine, who bore this burden rare
That I became, chomping at her imposed
And husband-tempered bit, upon her life:
Had she but known how worthy was this love
That freedom's song would sing in me, and rare,
And like a jewel—Diana in her orb—
She might yet have bestowed life on me more
And suffered all again that I had caused
Of anguish to her life, that she express
Her love in me and I mine in a song
The trees will sing as pages full of voice
For centuries to come, if voice be saved
For language tilled upon these decades here
That we *have* crossed and *will* while yet we search
To find survival and unendedness
To that which, lawful, I might not express
In handedness,[*] neutrino-like, but must,
Like ravens, only future's bounty trust,
   And brave Diana.

As Is Your Wont

Some flames are such that moths are driven *from*,
instead of to, sensing they will be scorched or singed,
 and such a flame am I. Therefore the braver seems
your being drawn to me at all, as was the case
when once, as worm, you sought my glowing ember's warmth,
and later when you fluttered near, drawn by the beacon
beckoning *naught but* you (by fate or by design).
Such courage stands the reason I remain transfixed
And beaming still, entranced by what that glow brought forth.

I'm covered now—a lantern white—and burn not wing
nor snout of any flying thing that flutters near.
But I am covered by a shade as well and this
remove only when wings I *know* are near, eyes

[*] *(neutrinos are 'left-handed', meaning the spin is as the fingers of the left hand where the thumb indicates the direction of motion) (anti-neutrinos are right-handed)*

whose light has *braved* my warmth: I seek to waste no sheen
upon ought else, as if to thus conserve the finite
fuel remaining. But brave one need no-longer be;
for I am covered now—a lantern white—and burn
not wing nor snout of any flying thing about.
You thus may wing your way to me at fancy's 'hest,
Safely to wing away—once more—as is your wont,
Safely to wing away.

As Air or Feet

Think you not that I think not of you
my every waking moment from *indifference!*
Is that what makes me well up in these ducts
that empty out the eyes? Nothing is seen
when thoughts of you are standing in my sight
and next to nothing heard nor touched when wraiths
of your soft breath hover about as if
to almost brush my cheek, caress my shoulder.
Can you not fathom that you are my life
yet being so have fled to quarters east
and north? I'm not as strong without your breath
beating beside me, even if just in spirit,
your eyelids trained on others. *These* as *well*
I love: *any* being you have smiled
upon or with is family to me,
cherished as much as air. Or feet. Or time.

I Warm My Hands in the Whirlpool

There is the Cauldron in your very voice
That summons me from regions of remorse
To where it's warm and shaded, cool and bright,
And can be mixed an ardent, potent brew
That charms the skins off dragons in the night.

[*Poems from here on she has not seen.*]

Across a Shaded Brook

I wore one of my feathers from the olden days
tonight whilst I traversed my way about the town.
It's worn here on the right-hand side, to send you word
(across thousands of miles, I guess, though close in thought)
what's fresh sprung from the depths of me, whose waters swell
that once bathed me in blessedness, then later chose
to perch loftily, lifted to exalted calm
beyond levels where cloud and mist obscure the view,
equipped (armed) with the patience of that wily bug
the dung beetle or scarab, with its ball (the sun)
of gold made from the droppings of some giant beast
as on (onwards) it pushes this until it reach
the hearth next to the heart of things. It's towards this goal
that life struggles; but now it struggles patiently,
its task buoyed by thoughts of your expressive face
and warm spirit of calm regard, whose humor spills
like bright bubble-ing swirls across a shaded brook.

On the Eve of the Weekend in Their Honor

    The sun is glowing silver
    and sinking downward slowly,
    as if the air were smoky,
    while ever onward, solely
    shouldering what we shun,
    it soldiers ever on.

    Do heroes' grow more hallowed
    by how we see them? wholeness
    exemplified? unfallow?
    exacting freedom from us?
    showing us what is won
    by soldiering ever on?

The sun this eve is silver
and setting: ever seaward
it sinks yet wrests no solace
from rest but races round us
to shoulder what we shun,
soldiering ever on.

The Kick

The moon has the shape of a football tonight.
     Hell of a kick.
Reflected, its light then reflects off the sea—
     Hell of a trick!—
Then flies right at me, who has verse for a soul:
     Hell of a pick
Since words can affect what the hearer might do.
     Hell of a kick.

Man's Crisp Rudeness

The moon, full, hides
in thin cloud, torn
between tried want
and dark, clear sight
of man's lamed will.
The light's orb *could*
reveal stark truths.
Instead clouds veil
the rich prize held
in trust whilst man
ascends, climbs clear
of fogged crude vales
and lifts eyes' gaze
to peer *past* veils
to grasp truths fixed

and *un*stopped, held
in trust, stemmed *not*
by fear's sad glimpse
of man's crisp rudeness.

My Mistress, Absent Me

She's like a new Prokofiev symphony every day—
    Even sleeping, she's like Bach,
    Although I've never *seen* her sleep.
Like the near half-moon in the sky tonight,
She can tip and nothing slips away.

That is how I see her in the mind's eye—
Not memory, but rather the timeless way of her
That makes the way I seek and makes the way she speaks
For me to hear and makes the way she breathes at me
    When I breathe back:
That is what makes the symphony her fragrance is,
    Since it is hers,
That is what heals the beast in me to make the man,
    The man I am becoming now,
    The man I am become.

The Distant Diana

    There in the teal blue of dusk,
    it seems as if the other half
    of the moon's disk should block sky *out;*
    but all I see is its *lit* half
    where sky opens to let it pass.
    The moon must be *above* the sky
    in what they call 'the heavens'. If only *I*
    could be up there beside the moon tonight,
        I'd be in heaven.

The Alien Man[*]

O. Gee. Look. It's streets.
And flat things. Hard things.
Whupty doo. Look. More of them.
Streets. And hard men. Look.
And hard women, too. Hard
People. O, and soft victims.
Look. And the prized peacock roams
Zoos no more. It's too crowded,
Here. And too open, there.
And just right somewhere in
Between the two. Whupty doo.

Two, three: look! see.
Find the hard things, one-two-three.
Climb the railings, jump free.
One, two; one three.

And the wild, ambling nothings,
And the tame, rooted ones . . .
And the wild, ambling ones,
And the tame, rooted nothings . . .

How like a rock shall I say it is, this 'life'?

The Alien Man sees life
Through the haze of the world.

Beyond Eighteen
(addressed to myself)

The forty other sails have set
over daffodils.
The fifteen other fancy feasts
sulfur has slain,

---

[*] meaning the Gnostic (such as myself), whose 'God' is often referred to as 'the alien God'

and this two lumps ago. The field
lies fallow.

The snow is leaped. The ridge tunneled;
all otherwise.
The fifteen seldom sumptuous shells
bypassed.
For we are on the other side
of nothing now.
We are in the grip of snows
purely internal.

We are where the track has fled
feetingly, entreatingly,
and yet unmarked. Fold! featherweight:
I hold the cards that foot you down
to the void
of the Otherworld
(which seems a void to you at least).

There is no place a file can flee
that's not a place,
whereas a rasp can make a void
in which to hide.
(Now that I've led you up the slope,
don't slide.)

The Moon Will Set Things Right

A striking light in the sky tonight:
      It is the moon.
It vaulted up not long ago,
      None too soon.
The sky was empty for a while . . .
      There *are* no stars—
Except the memory of them,
      And sometimes Mars
And Venus, of course, and Jupiter

Suitably bright—
Mostly the emptiness of the inner
And outer night,
And then the moon:
The *moon* will set things right.

Encased in Cold
[*Wreathed Cyhydedd Fer 'Sonnet'*]

Encased in cold, a mind can shake
what shakes and keep, for mem'ries' sake,
what is forsaken, an ice pack
packed on the wound time's present tack
has tacked on life, which takes its toll
untold, through deaths unsung: the soul,
sole witness to it, keeps it in,
for in it nothing can begin.
Beginning, there are only ends,
not ends we've sought but endings, bends
whose bent leads back into the past
past reasons to the *cause* at last:
that last mistake, which if unmade
would not have made all bright hope fade.

R i p p l e s

The ripples of high ice clouds vast in scope
dwarf the salted mountain peaks.
Underneath them a plane descends
makes its approach to land.
How, then, can the thoughts of a man
not even six feet tall
dwarf all these things?
For *my* thoughts reach clear to a galaxy's distant hub,
and I am one of the least traveled
among men.

Truly amazing, until you realize
that gravity doesn't slow *thoughts* down.
Still, they do have to generate
their own electricity
just like a galaxy,
quite a feat for a pair of feet with a head!

Pull Not My Heart

The elements that gather about my eyes
and ears and body, empty of their spell,
pull not my heart. I send an empty stare
in their direction, while I look instead
with steadfast gaze at what I have become
that wishes no entanglement with life
save where the love I savor walks and breathes.
And since her steps are not where I can hear,
the warm air of her words not near enough to feel
pounding upon my skin, I simply play the eel
and slither far beneath the surf that seethes
with self-important things as they appear.

Suspended

Drawn out over a continent of leagues
in league with separation is this wrong
I'm wrong to blame on one poor fool's intrigues,
intriguing though they were. Those wiles are gone.
Gone are the days, not years, that made apt seeds
to seed such sense of absence: stretched from pawn
to pawn, the players' touch slips close like weeds
unweeded in this meadow where they're drawn.

The Silent Fountain

Deep in a dream of solace made of jade
no sound that surfaced made distraction known
nor splash of wake nor surf oft stiffly blown
upon a shore turned numb, which life had flayed
with storms unnumbered through which thought might wade
almost unseeing there where it had flown
to find itself both less and more alone,
solitude's void of old a friend new-made.
Then, the still air its long-awaited cue,
a lush and ornate fountain, framed in green
and flowing always, could at last appear
that needs no din of gurgling to imbue
with sparkling richness what's beneath its sheen
to quench the eternal thirst that I hold dear.

Crown of Sonnets: The Darkness of the Wind

The darkness of the wind heart's sails demand
if moments are to have their hoplite's shield
of convex might against the barbs you wield—
whose iron is doubt, o mistress of time's sand—
is like a storm's approach, the shadowed land
no haven, no dim sun beyond concealed
to reappear somehow once all is healed,
for that is not the gentleness at hand.
Rather it is the long surcease that beckons
beyond the rim of life, to await the gong
that summons mind *to* life when fondness threatens
to be renewed again, however long
the gap from this day's hurt to that which reckons
wealth is in worth of being, not of song.

Wealth is in worth of being, not of song,
we tell ourselves, and yet man's wind-starved ears
still crave song's notes to calm his crouching fears
by fielding the illusion we 'belong'

and do not stand alone but in a throng,
a myriad sinning souls, whose brandished spears
of accusation 'prep' us for our biers . . .
but no, I'm by myself when I do wrong.
No shoulder-blades but mine can bear this load
I make by my mistaken ways, wrong turns,
and evil thoughts: what day is it? today?
then brave new weight's been added to the goad
that tries to turn aside the bull that yearns
to make its own unmediated way.

To make its own unmediated way—
prerogative of kings, of gods, of *weather*,
but not of men—is goad's mirage, whose tether
forces the present on the unwilling, grey,
and color-challenged gloom, in which we stay
because we do not *rule* the sky, each feather
within our wings a seat of burnished leather
within this dungeon's night in which we bray.
For stubborn is as stubborn does, an anger
aimed at the pull of night upon each morn
that's clipping short the hours until the dawn.
No wagon waits to cart off heads; for languor
replaces seething will once will is shorn,
its innocence the purview of the fawn.

Its innocence the purview of the fawn,
momentum—from the play of fantasies
upon the brain-tied mind—makes its own breeze
and sings to sleep the things that now are gone
yet wakens with its whistling spark the spawn
of thought-creation—chains and future keys
imprisoning us by freeing travesties
from ownership by those who would move on.
So we must backtrack often, having left
such islands of resistance in our wakes
as cannot stand the tears of the bereft
nor take the false serenity of lakes
when gales aloft beckon: whole strings of deft
excuses cannot stem the tide wrong makes.

Excuses cannot stem the tide wrong makes
when overriding conscience. Moon and sun
and myriad stars align themselves on one
instructive axis, slamming on the brakes
and holding waters fast till motion aches
to free again their massive flow, begun
by lusting after prizes never won
because their sheen is pure and we but rakes.
Whatever slakes one's thirst for brave adventure
may calm the heart a while, but pulse returns
(with birth) to once more batter us with censure,
the high self hoping its delinquent learns
those lessons' thrusts our throbs of lust indenture
our spirits to, however much it burns.

Our spirits, too—however much it burns—
partake in being fooled by what the will
that conjured them perceives as ought or nil
that led it on this journey's path, which worms
complete decomposition of, by turns
its janitor and food for crows: we spill
our blood for something or for nothing, kill
the hunted goatherd, and make oil of ferns.
Long ages, æons—hosts of pulse-like breaths—
have passed and will yet pass before the truer
sun that's *behind* the sun can broach this heaven
that is man's hell, to drain it of its deaths
and mark its ocean's depths, a great renewer
this once immortal flour itself must leaven.

This once immortal flour *itself* must leaven
the mortal blob it has become; transform
through alchemy this flesh from dying norm
to living aberration; *climb* the seven
all-spanning palace steps from Gaul or Devon
that reach the Inner Kingdom—what's not born
but latent in the eye of passion's storm.
(Once nature's *four* adjust, 'twill be *eleven*.)
Each birth yields one more chance: but lives get squandered

on spreading out more minefields for the future,
transforming seas into a barren land.
I know this yet away from youth have wandered,
led by this wound you are, its only suture
the darkness of the wind heart's sails demand.

Fifteen Line Sonnet in Tetrameter

I have a damaged sense of time:
one year, two years, three years past,
I couldn't say: nothing much mine
has time affected by its grasp.
I have a damaged sense of time,
but now its thread is clipped in two,
cut by this lofty lonesome pine
the air about which misses you.
Yet pine transposes into fir
to herald a rebirth not far
from where our lofty notions were
when once again we think we are
that now pretend to be, and there
amidst the mists we pierce for her
will time my damaged sense repair.

My Inner Devotion: The *Shekhinah*

It's quite an odd experience to pledge
chastity to myself still as enamored
of one as I have ever been—no hedge,
merely the pulse by which my heart is hammered.
An untranslatable, transmuted need
imprisons me by bond of her soft kiss,
by memories of words, on which I feed,
accustomed to desiring what's amiss.
For though she's wedded to another role,
her light remains the queen of my domain;

though time and entropy exact their toll,
no sign suggests this want may flag or wane;
platonic, though, in substance must it be
henceforth, till re-existence sets us free.

What Her Dearness Preached
[Sapphic Ode Sonnet]

There was no cushion where I fell
To tell my bones the world went on,
Yet everywhere your gentle spell
    Had left its spawn.
And lest ungathered waste remain
To clutter heart's insistent clamor,
I concentrated on the gain,
    Not loss, of glamour.
As you were now a land I'd won
Yet lost, *I* a country conquered then
Enthralled, the tale seemed sure to stun
    What might have been.
Life has not failed me; for I have reached
That triumph's end your dearness preached.

Remembered Voice
[Awdl Gywydd with cynghanedd]

Voice that does not pound choices
into ears says now to rise
above storm's shove, steer aims short
of ire's port. Mind veers. (Weep, eyes.)

The Residue
[Englyn Milwr with cynghanedd]

Though your will another warms,
I, since tossed in unceased storms,
see your lone face sire all forms.

Scent of the Past
[Séadna]

Scented prize of thought, you thunder
     under brown eyes, gently wrought.
Borne on wind's caress, you render
     stormlessness, tenderly taught.

Round your distant dance mine wanders,
     endures angst of the mind's mist,
this to keep from taint of taverns
     deep traces your caverns kissed.

Sun's returnings bring their blessings'
     ring of younger yearning's bent.
Swelling sense has found me favored,
     spellbound by your savored scent.

The You Within Me

With me you are: all the babble
     about hardly has a say.
I, my laugh, my tear, your temple
     here beneath your simple sway.

Though I know your dawns lie distant,
     spent night longs to list you close.
With lips' kiss that roused not recent,
     my licks miss their decent dose.

Part of you is in me always,
      bracing limbs you left to lie
empty of their molded meaning,
      lent them: cold they, singing, sigh.

How those winds of why go whistling
      even now through mist and moon,
teaching the sun's lure its limits'
      reach, a cure to dim its doom.

Who needs daylight when soft silver
      lurks aloft by night—dreams' sieve—
and hope's fluorescent wake, wonder,
      coats with shape the one you're with.

Treasure

Treasure to me that I have glimpsed your face
in more than just one circumstance of fate,
have spied your wry amusement at life's grace
or satisfaction at what filled your plate;
treasure, that imprints of your soft-spun voice
and barb still chide me while I brave this void,
that echoes of your breath make clear the choice
to garner calm when ruffled, churned, annoyed.
What greater treasure would it be to tread
beside your feet this path, to be your bless'd
receptor, gather in what you have said
fresh in these ears—for which the words were pressed—
and know that in the twilight of my day
your own might drink these poems that I say.

[See also pp. 125, 153, 188, 191-2, 196, 205, 209, and poems 1, 3, 4, & 6 starting on p. 181.]

B a r d

Old Forms
[Deibhidhe]

Timely song, whose special spark
consumes life's quests, mind's monarch,
weave words to a patterned pace
and leave great verse, like Lovelace.

Tradition's means mark the mold
the ear gleans, words' stark stronghold.
Naught so warms my socks to see
as old forms, taut and timely.

Straight Steps
[*Cyhydedd Hir*]

Straight steps the cold bard from his hidden, hard
life in this bold shard of what once blazed.

Old recalled greatness these times miss much less
once mankind's late mess makes us amazed.

Still, with this deep call heard, though in dim fall,
words want to leap tall in flame unfazed.

Sift out the coarse drum's thrum—makes my ears numb!
Bran, let my horse come forth, songs be raised!

An Old School Droighneach

Ah, the butter o' me tongue's pearly putterin'
utterin' unsurly wisdom purringly:
If't's what ye'r after, since I'm no slow, slumberin'
butt o' laughter left wonderin', I'll start stirringly.

Speechwise, nuthin's a nearly sa lyrical
spiritchal ear-stuffin' west *ar* east o' Italy
than an Irish lilt, seldom cynical,
in that stylish, spherical tongue Brits speak brittle-ly.

'Tis fluid an' thurrst-quenchin' under ahr tutelage,
a scruple-less drenchin' utherwise, I'm allegin'.
The way Celts handle English is a sweet synthesis.
(We've a fleeter angle on emphasis assessin'.)

'Tshould never be even a little bit lackluster
nor a blockbuster o' spittle, this mind musterin'.
Shahrly ya prafers hearts ta be all a-flutter—
ah, the butter o' me tongue's peahrly putterin'!

Asian
Poetry Forms

[*front yard haiku*]

wind through birch leaves
white roses flecked with red
cutting edge

[*dancing haiku*]

willow gushes
a spring in its step
waves off stillness

[*lowku*]

blind intensity of day
skin and bark challenged
worms cannot locate the stars

[Haiku (1 spring, 3 summer, 2 autumn)]

smoothed pebble
moss-covered joint of stick
brief torrent

almost steaming rain
punctuated by thunder
a heated lecture

concrete meadow
bark leaves twigs at rest
urban entropy

dry riverbed
still wind burning sun
moisture on skin

grapes sag
ivy snakes entwine
cling to stiffness

breeze stirs the aspen
damp sky billowing after
allies in mayhem

[subversive haiku]

earth's poles are tilted
leaves'll soon turn in color
this orb we're on's drunk!

[haiku after Æsop]

the humble reed
an internal wind
untouched

[haiku in vertical line with gaps]

narrow
trunk

leans
into
wind

s l o w
d a n c e

Broken Tea-Break
[senryu]

even the rugged
like delicate cups of tea
to sip between rugs

[senryu of adversity]

both torch and kindling
chose not to stay and stare
at the ruins

[senryu on living in a world gone mad]

> flame falters
> spirited away
> take me too

[self-referent senryu]

> prickly concrete
> soft flesh stern reason
> no echoes

[cork-horse senryu]

> how many bottles
> must I consume to construct
> a complete dragon

[animal composer senryu]

> moose-orgsky
> soused but not plastered
> on car bumpers

[drunkenryu]

> Lisssen, buddhy,
> Iwzsposed to go some-wares . . .
> Juno the place?

[backwards (Aurignacian) senryu]

man in the throes of an elk
painted on earth-sky
to control the buffalo

Ominous Flower
[*Tanka*]

ominous flower
casts an encroaching shadow
on the worms below
who shiver in expectation
of the sun sliding into night

How Grass Affects Its Betters

grass gets on the nerves
of ash while alder adores
lawn's brash rebounding
the plucky perseverance
of ingrained subservience[*]

Tanka You Very Much

innocuous eyes
eerily project their calm
on the world's thunder
which stares back dumbstruck and still
after its current is spent

---

[*] hat-tip to the alder god Bran being cognate with Scandinavian Fro, patron of royalty

The Coming-of-Age of the Mind
[in the Thai form called Kloon or Klon]

Sights that stun with wonder unseen:
seventeen, mind green, not yet tilled,
light looms just where lust's quake is stilled,
unfulfilled, strong-willed, poised to spin.

Thus begin sanguine, wanton spurts
past culverts where hurt's hand was felt
into fields where thought had not dwelt
nor knees knelt yet shelter beckons.

Emotion's factions must unhand
to expand where grandeur seeps close,
secrets' antidote to morose
thoughts' engrossing dose of what blocks.

Youth's pulse rocks old locks: mind's hungers
are what stirs embers of what's cast
in breaking through to where things last,
in contrast to pastimes' vast sights.

Muse of Twilight
[in the Vietnamese form called Luc Bat]

In the in-between time,
when light turns on a dime—that cusp
bordering the dull husk
of night, whose inward thrust accosts
our blocks and mental frosts—
are rich moments when costs matter
not and the mad hatter
shuns phrases that flatter for that
which wouldn't stir a cat
from sleep but cuts the slat that blocks
our seeing through the shocks
that have us on the rocks to thus

appreciate the fuss
our fathers made for us serving
times unknown by swerving
around the unnerving squalor
of poor notions, ardor
saved to reduce pallor from lips
cold with repeated trips
to where life's cauldron dips down low
to allow the still flow
of craft life's shutters show in full
as the mind tries to pull
its version of thick wool across
its own eyes' gathered moss
so as to then emboss the soon
ensuing day with noon
unglaring in its swoon, the bright
words brimming with calm might
night's sub-ambient light might mime.

Cambodia
[Pathya Vat]

Reflect, stilled face
swan's soaring neck
that sways to check
if others care.

Quiet prevails
as morning's spare
dance turns its air
to jeweled eyes.

The land is rich
with broken ties
where silent cries
of massed skulls quake.

A GoVat Lament

Contrive, if you can, to conceive
just what it is for which they grieve
who recall glib airs of folly.

Each great notion's ghost that must leave,
whose arm fits not the top-down sleeve,
recalls the glib airs of folly.

Sobs importune each latest peeve
to spare those whom its moves bereave
that have borne glib airs of folly.

But wisdom's gems the lost retrieve
only once there is no reprieve
from the fruits of glib airs' folly.

By Arrangement with Strangeness
[YaDu]

Was it from doubt,
this about face
you tout now, torn
by forlorn grace
whose storm you were trying to erase?

Yes, souls do change,
by arrangement
with strangeness, god
of the prod, sent
by oddness to say what normal meant.

Silhouetted
and fêted, wants
vetted, we rise
till our eyes find
where guise feels at home again and kind.

Formula For Uplift of Sad Souls

Can the shadowed
input mode made
windowed and bade
not be sad slip
past glad tidings into its cold castle's grip?

No, fear not, since
the ripe quince shall
evince tongue's smile
and beguile frown's
cramped style that would depopulate its own downs.

Pantoum Schmantoum

This business of requiring lines repeat
and yet mean something diff'rent when they do?
To write a good pantoum: a priceless feat!
(undoable but by a precious few).

And yet mean something diff'rent when they do?
How does one make the same old words spring fresh?
Undoable! but by a precious few.
And the repeated lines must intermesh!

How does one make the same old words spring fresh
as if from new-turned soil plowed long ago?
And the repeated lines must intermesh!
Repeated tries, with nothing yet to show.

As if from new-turned soil plowed long ago?
To even *say* this paints me quite the fool.
Repeated tries with nothing yet to show—
the fees must be quite steep at pantoum school!

To even *say* this paints me quite the fool:
I doubt if I will *ever* see the light!

The fees must be quite steep at pantoum school.
(A fool's errand! a waste of mental might!)

I doubt if I will *ever* see the light.
To write a good pantoum a priceless feat?
A fool's errand! a waste of mental might!
this business of requiring lines repeat.

Ghazal and the Night Visitors

The contest for my attention has been held already,
and the forest of what escaped has been felled already.

Calm's vastness waits to assert itself on a troubled sea
till an hour after the wind's rage has been belled already.

Sincerely untroubled perks eyes' gleam among fleet creatures
as the short tree with legs goes by, deep thoughts quelled already.

Sometime symptoms of passion's sickness fail in their ambush
if the infection of youth's abscess has swelled already.

The dreamer in me strives to paint an adequate signpost
but cannot recall how the key word was spelled already.

Quality among clouds often starts out underrated
then suddenly wished for when thunder has knelled already.

The average content of man's many decades appears,
upon reflection in calm pools, to have jelled already.

And meanwhile the mad poet of Venice Beach has been barred
from contentment with no recourse, having yelled already.

Not being a woman under Taliban oppression, I do not include any example of Landay, an often bawdy, usually satirical couplet never (at risk of life) recited in presence of men. Nor do I delve into the quantitative morass of Shloka, common form of Sanskrit poetry and proverb. But I have dabbled in quantitative Greek and Roman meters, for pure enjoyment. The following are attempts at imitating same.

Quantitative Meters

(Greek & Roman)

The World Without
[Second Asclepiadean]

Con-game launched by the cold platoon
Mankind lost in a maze mindfully made for it
Not quite weaned of a bold excuse
Oft unhinged by its face, crushed by the wind of it
Roused here. Ought that enhanced the breeze
Holds chained all but the rare flour that escaped the loaf.

Rendering Greek Meter in English
[Sapphic Stanza]

Couched in wind's blithe speech, the behest of moonbeams
stokes the tongue's wide reach to include the gentler
modes composed long past by a younger mankind,
    versed in the wind's source.

Shall the kind gods dance? are the tendrils tended?
watched? adorned? kept moist? or is time a bandit
poised to rob lush ways of a chance to bloom here,
        wounded by darkness?

Rules are not much help. For a word that one way
rings a long drawn-out and sustained exposure,
once arranged else-wise can dissolve to shortness,
        clipped by the context.

Only whilst one strives with a constant mindset
tuned to sounds called forth by the words and phrases
springs the best close sketch of the ancient stanzas'
        steps of composure.

Bard, relax not yet! Let the storms that rise here,
poised to lure tongue's way, be revered: a contract
passed to years yet young, for the ears attending
        plead to be danced with!

Melpomene Speaks

Cry the ramparts lost in a wakeful abstract
drawn to ears stretched wide by a name that lingers
long a-masked, once fair, though for now anointed
        weed of the wasteland.

Pray lament once well the approach to godhead
walked in trust's own gait by the rich in manhood
lured aloof, where pain, the attendant glow-worm,
        lights with its fogged breath.

Sing in maze-bound steps what is danced to limelight
shone on wills not bowed by the flagrant riffraff
spawn of mundane winds, who attack the noblest,
        borne on conceit's wave.

Wail, a voice unleashed; for the ancient fabric—
spun by men gods wove, in the path of doomsday,
past chagrin's veiled shock, into cloth that's timeless—
      hangs on a tale's hook.

Find, in unschooled times, the device to vanquish
airs the noblest shun: the ungrateful whine's song
poured from hearts not strong. In the void, arise now,
      bristling a war-cry!

Helen of Troy Speaks
[Dactylic Hexameter]

Winds of a thousand storms have cast forth doom on a princess
shorn proper choice by the tyrant gods whose wills are unquestioned!
Shall I obey such gods, whose care isn't roused by a weakling?
Take beauty's curse from a soul not accustomed yet to attention
tuned to appraise my plight as if *I* were the cause of destruction!
Fate's callous hand has encumbered accomplices caught in a tragic
jest! for the place I was brought cannot hope to prevail over warriors
bent upon hate's savage end: to assail Troy's long unimpeached walls
just to return me to harsh Agamemnon's vale of protection.
Would that a dart from the bow of a prince might cut the Achilles
tendon of him who has slain great Hector and dragged his remains off!
Fixed upon vengeance, Greeks bearing gifts might act as Cassandra
warns, though we heed not: sealed are the fortunes war has bequeathed us!
Bards, in an age long since, may rightly remember, in grieving,
wonders we held within ramparts manned by the brave, who were ground down
hard by the boot of deceit in the hands of the gods on their high horse.

Catharsis in Our Times

Life's purpose lurks in the sea-swept depths that are stirred as we pass through.
Time's murky content swirls all about, so the light as it swoops down
soft from above can at least touch each of its broad surface textures,
test what it is, get a reasonable context, *see* where it comes from.

Soft is a life not lived where boisterous wars everlasting
call forth strength in the soul's force, force tears' fount of bereavement
forth from us all, thoughts filled full of grim understanding of hardship
sprung out of heartfelt loss, or acquired in the midst of the conflicts
waged over fields long sown with the blood of the brave and the valiant.

Thus, though our lives flow sweetly and tongues can imbibe of it meekly,
still there's a path to be had that allows for a tale to be garnished,
patched, even filled with a drill that the soul needs: clouds on a clear day,
fierce battle's din in the midst of the wiles underneath all the bland smiles.

Minds fully bent to appraise what the world shows *and* what it hides well
grow when a lifetime's worth of aroused fear, danger, and conflict
wax vivid *while yet* peace and contentment reign—in a film, say,
picturing sad loss, pains that can stem from a failure, a bad choice,
scenes into which suffering, and a sense of the depth of the world's well
whence can be drawn life's sourness, *gets* to us, rends our contentment.

Fear helps thought probe deep into realms that our needs as they drive us
must understand to survive. For without such forced exercise, life's
vesture of bold cunning wanes. Let élan, with its cloak of attendant
firmness of grand purposes when conceived to a backdrop of hardship's
face, let it move us! Themes can be made to evoke from us greatness
drawn from the depths of enthrallment in tales out of times and comportments
not like our own. What a useful tool this culture bequeaths us!

Mouthful

Onward I float, on a sea that's becalmed, to enjoin the encroachments
spawned of deprived times kindly to loose their hold on my lifestyle.
Where are the oars that I need! and the arms whose pull is deliv'rance!
I am a wind of the sea, says the ash; truth's boar is the alder:
how might one lone voice harmonize with itself in the first place!
Well do I know what you hear comes close, does it not, to a mouthful?

Rowing Meter

Anglo-Saxon Strong-Stress Alliterative Verse
[further examples on pp. 19 & 22]

Storm Vision

What will, I wonder,
    waken the starlight
that glowed in your eyes
    ever from the north
when together once we lingered
    looking for the answer
to each other's asking
    on the edge of day?
What will, I wonder,
    waken that white fire
that shone in the night sky
    as the North Star shines
when night creeps round us
    and the need is near
for a fixed point to follow
    over the fathoms of a life?
With the firelight of your eyes
    before me as I sailed,
my hands were unheeded
    and the helm followed
of its own accord
    the course you set for it.

But after I was far
    out to sea,
your beacon-light faltered
    and forth from the deep
came storm-driven champions
    of cheerlessness and woe.
Things that had always
    offered solace,
things that I had loved,
    that were life-giving,
rose up around me
    and in a wrath of ugliness
became ungodly
    goblin shapes,
mighty and monstrous
    man-devourers
that came at me as I watched
    or waited in shadows
for me to behold,
    horror-stricken.
In vain I cast
    cries of fearfulness,
unheeded words
    that were wind-swallowed
and fell on the empty
    ears of the night.
Slowly I steadied
    my storm-ridden ship
and shut out the cavernous
    cackling around me
and noticed that the seething
    of that senseless storm-tumult
was spawned out of my own
    despair and grief.
Lost and directionless,
    lonely and chill-beset,
I had imagined clouds
    to cover the seeming
emptiness of the sky,
    and out of those hovering

apparitions of doom
      the darkness sprang:
the insane, wrathful
      writhing of the sea
grew out of the shadows
      that had gripped my world.
For without that wondrous star
      that once had guided me
over the ocean,
      it was as if no other stars shown.
No shimmering daylight
      danced upon the waves
from moon or otherwhere
      and all at once
fell a great darkness
      from the sky
like condors swooping
      with a sudden cry,
their black wings blotting out
      all bliss and brightness.
Your eyes no longer
      lingered in my gaze
like beads of smiling
      sun-like rapture
as they had before
      but fell away in fear
when I sought them. Not even
      one echo remained
of their bright calling.
      What can, I wonder,
waken that starlight
      that waits no longer
sweet-tongued in twilight
      for the touch of my hand
and the coming of my ship
      to its shore?

'To Lady Lord'

Wary and watchful
      walk they still
in the threatening twilight
      of trust-unworthiness
while the earth-winter
      of an age dying
weeps its unceasing
      sorrow in our ears
and asks the timeless
      answerless questions
of dying mankind
      a mortal species
amid immortal
      monkey organisms
that plague the universe
      with patternless ignorance
of death and ending.
      Damn the torpedoes
of self turned self-ward
      stabbing and rending
with learning turned bomb-ward
      blind to being
in the night when nobody
      notices anything
beyond their own
      ugly noses.

Glass Goblets

Glass goblets
      and gifted manners
are the pulled pages
      of past and future
where fools frolic
      in phantom wishes
and faith falters

in fortune's mazes,
those long labyrinths,
     leaky, twisting.
Rain ravenous,
     wrath of heaven:
soak to the soul
     the seamy serpent!
For muffled music
     mocks the deafening
thud of thunder
     from thatched houses.
Vulnerable vases
     reveal their contents
only to the visions
     of the versed.

Bones of the Great Whale

Towering tunnel,
     your tendon-less, well-windowed
ribs alone rob us
     of regal stature.
I hear something within them
     that hies to the wind's cadence:
an unlabored litheness,
     a little-known efficiency
buoyed and borne up
     by the best of what surrounds you.

Who Await

I arose as a riddle-to-myself
     riding upon the war-steed
of the realization
     that riotous fun awaits me
as well as pain. The whimpering
     of my own whales behind me,
where beasts of lesser fortune

have found their extinction,
hovers as a reminder
    that the hives keep on gathering
and the question still remains:
    is this man one of the worthless
who await, or one of the weightless
    who a-worth?

The Dancing Maya

The dancing *maya*
    darkens with glamour
the scene I forge
    with festering design
in my blacksmith mind,
    the makings of happiness
were I not the only one
    interested. Faltering,
I gather up courage,
    again. Hesitant,
still I can't afford
    to be fickle: no moment
must pass that is not paved
    with purpose most steadfast.
Oblivion beckons
    obliquely, and I will not
be party to it. Self-same
    sentence has been passed
on the fool as on the cunning
    without character, who is aimless
as water without wind:
    wisdom is the current's source.

Shaped
&
Syllabic

Hourglass
[*A Mirrored Reverse Etheree*]

Seemingly timeless love which used to bask
in the faint glimmer of once bright hope
in the past not once shirked its task
nor failed to grant lust the rope
to hang himself with coils
of long welcome toils
to serve its wiles
now defiles
its calm
balm
need
to bleed
turbid tears
caught in arrears
escapes and wends on
as thoughts no longer fawn
quite where the same altar lurks
since being torn by love's clear light
that deceives not, that's not how it works
love lays its truths out bold as black and white

Seer Seeing Beyond Space
[*Lanturne plus Tetractys*]

once
or twice
in the space
of ten lifetimes
clouds

part
and eye
sees beyond
scattered reports
of gold whose light lurks in the high reaches

Nature Versus Thought
[*Septolet*]

Months
crawling by
on leaves' wings
fly

slowly by
reordered
by the mind's eye.

Bullet I Dodged (Having Entered This Body Subsequent to Its Being *One*)
[*Cinquain*]

infant
no questions yet
yet it complains a lot
constant source of irritation
noise blob

Short-Lived

In rapt
attention held,
the butterfly ignored
its brief, colorful life and just
fluttered.

Winged Brain
[Butterfly Cinquain]

flitting
about the yard
cerebral colors stirred
this waking up to smell the air
pitting
image against the bushes there
in a shape to be heard
so it's not hard
sitting

Changes
[Rictameter]

changes
ensnare the mind
in steep mountain ranges
from finding what cannot now find
what it was before and that what's in store
looms lost as the old garish grind
masks what time deranges
with ill-designed
changes

Perhaps

[Hexaduad]

Perhaps
the naps
forced on me as a child
led my mind to go wild
because it does not seem to move
along in quite so smooth a groove
as fashion's cue.
How about you?
does normal seem to be
as weird as 'twas to me?
Don't answer that:
you're just a c a t !

Sight Blinds

[Inverted Hexaduad]

Sight blinds
the most perceptive minds
as they struggle to make some sense
of present tense.

They have been told the air
is all that's there,
yet the mind's Light
is not a *thing* of sight.

No gag muzzles
the shout of time: it still puzzles
the most perceptive minds
sight blinds.

The Dark Lighthouse
[Shadorma (Spanish)]

fathoms churn
soul out of its depth
seeks a course
of wholeness
not engendered by the crowd
of sing-song sirens

the sea stills
wake the calm of death
helm now free
where sails flap
for want of one line drawn taut
to give it fair wind

Calm Needed
[Trois-par-Huit]

go ye bards
amongst the sylphs and stars
to transmit the message that spirit

has essence more real than the objects that fear it
suspecting that that is what moves them when near it

the breath quickens from being heated
blandness is defeated
calm needed

Trees

vegetation distribution
birch rowan and ash at high altitudes
alder and willow where land descends
hawthorn hedges about the hearth
oak and holly vie for rule
hazel feeds salmon
vine and ivy
entwine
trunks
reeds
cling to
waterways
funereal elder

Man

Man
Suffers
More than beasts
Who are blissful
And have no anger
Even when they falter
Following after
Man where his axe
Fell upon
Feasting
Trees

Mighty are the sparrows
Even as the arrow's
Sharp-taloned thrust
Whisks them into dust

Rispettos

Summer

Reveal the tumult of the earth
resounding underneath your breast
with tender-hearted hues of mirth
and nature's course will do the rest.

These paragons of form, once scent,
confirm it is your grace that lent
the world its spirit of delight
and warmth that courses through the night.

The Gypsy Dancer

Mark where the girl, the camp-follower,
Seeks to seduce the fatigued of war.
Myself she only drills hollower—
She swirls, as do my mates no more.

I'll give her gifted, though: she sways
And hypnotizes with her ways
Of calling us, through gentle motion,
From here across war's weighty ocean.

Freedom's Twin Faces
[*Heroic Rispetto*]

In consequence of having gone too far,
His days are spent not far from where he sleeps,
For freedom's own quintessence is the star
Of self-restraint, whose faith the wise man keeps.

For absent a restraining inner wall
Must wall *without* rear up; and though a stall
May be the proper setting for a horse,
We hominids should seek a better course.

Triple Huntress: Fir, Heather, Yew

The night has carved a slender bow of fir,
And seven days from now it will be strung:
'Tis then night's huntress, given light, will stir
To loose the feathered shaft (her poet's tongue).

The heath awaits, as huntress slowly pulls
And then releases, while its brightness dulls,
Transformed to yew-wood: shaft must find its mark
In silence, as the poet's eyes grow dark.

Sonnets
Italian Style

[You will also find eight of my better Petrarchans beginning on page 112 above.]

Some Paintings
[Sonnet Rispetto]

Some paintings: yes, let's take a look.
Oh my! Renoir, the very cream!
Two sisters studying a book—
how innocent and mild they seem!
Beyond that, God forbid I brook
to put in words what seems a dream:
if words described it well, what point
were paint except to but anoint!
And yet there's really not much room
within this form to wax verbose
about the qualities that loom
before us: thereby may its dose
of sweet rich hues escape, as doom,
my turning joyful lachrymose.

Where Truth's Wind Blew
[Petrarchan with homophone-framed lines]

Sole owner am I of this sorry soul,
hoarfrost on beard, that acts as nature's whore.
Pour out corruption's slag from every pore;
whole slates scrape clean: they leave no gaping hole.
Role that I've played, loose grip! while back I roll
or dodge each wave or with firm grip on oar
bore through this sea, snout down like rooting boar,
poll heeded not, my hand on fathoms' pole.
Lone user of this flesh I have on loan
do I but seek no more than what is due,
grown wiser (by design), no more to groan
to face life's pains as one instead of two:
shown *why* we fail, I rise, as if love shone
blue lit, since whitened, here where truth's wind blew.

The Mind's Girth
[Petrarchan]

The iceberg of thought's world sticks little peaks
of like attracting like through demon masks
we make of all the unattractive tasks
we've left ourselves, for we are what life seeks
(delayed by matter's stubbornness): time reeks
of cold illusion as each notion asks
to be dispensed into the little flasks
that moments are, until their new shelf creaks.
But in the echo of that cracking sound
is weight of meaning also, not of earth
alone, nor is that flask-collection bound
for anyone but us; for we are *worth*
the efforts nature makes and will astound
the heavens once our minds have found their girth.

Born Free I Wish!

"Man though born free is everywhere in chains,"
Rousseau declared: how faulty was his sight
to not have seen beyond sin's outer light
to karma's weight that waits within then rains
upon one's life, defining what are gains
and what losses according to the blight
which thoughts in former lives make recondite
or obvious adjustments to in grains.
What myriad existences we brave
(having no choice) *already* nailed to crosses
we don't remember, but they remember us:
we *made* them! prior to some former grave,
and now they lord it over us, like bosses
still sore because we missed the party bus.

After Fontenoy

We left the bloody field of Fontenoy
Dispirited chevaliers who had let
The Irish garner all ze crêpe suzette
Of glory, prompting us to think *pourquoi*
We white-clad French have not *je ne sais quoi*
Enough to stand and have a tête à tête
With British redcoats when they pirouette
Before our banks of cannons *un deux trois*.
Albeit once we got to gay Paree
Our makeshift hearts transcended their ennui—
It's easy with enough *concorde du place*,
For there's an endless fount of *corps d'esprit*
Where banks of femmes fatales are *très jolie*
And exquisite Bordeaux the coup de grace.

Self-Imposed Hardship

Intrinsic to the cavalcade of mires
our wagons can get stuck in is the pond
of quicksand made of muck our anger spawned
upon its being shoveled under tires
too often: old mules kick contagious fires
across campsites with which we've formed a bond
of memory or will, forging a fond
attachment thereto out of old desires.
Such depth is transferred to the looming bog
that leads to our undoing for the nonce,
its sinkings seeming insurmountable
until such time has passed as lifts the fog
and lets us see it is our own response
that overwhelms us with its downward pull.

Declining Times

Strange how the fin-fish in their shallow pond,
the little thin fish with transparent skins,
continue jumping into little tins
with spirits soaring like a vagabond
in seeking out those things of which they're fond
that dangle from the lines of mandarins,
and heedless of the hooks that sting like pins
go on about their business and beyond.
And the dim-shadowed, slender-fingered nails
extending finger length beyond their pads
exude the turbid hue of tangerines
to hide a nervous tapping that impales
as hands enclose the sky with hits and fads
and suction cups that swallow up our means.

Sonnets
English Style

Sufficient Insufficiency
[Wreathed Tetrameter]

Sufficient stress accosts my purse
(pursuing things that cost) that I
iconic'ly fulfill the curse
(or worse) incurred by birth: to cry
is cryogenic; yet to laugh
is laughable. What choice is left
that's right? Fearful of every gaffe—
or gaff that spears my heart—my heft
lacks heftiness. Yet now I turn
internal, where my thoughts are hexed
hexameter and I still burn
hibernal yet with love annexed.
Next best thing, if not omniscient?
Knowing I am insufficient.

Bird-Messenger
[*Shakespearean*]

Fly, little brother, you who can ascend
to heights I can't aspire to, where the spirit
of all that is exalted reigns: unbend
your wings and take this prayer where sky might hear it.
Address the winds aloft on man's behalf,
chill though they be, to let them know their mask
of majesty has not yet slipped nor laugh
derisive plagued the praise in which they bask.
Then ask if man's yet paid in full for being
deceived into believing *out* is *up*
or that the stars' coldness is worth the seeing
or sun's great bounty worthy of man's cup.
Fly, little brother, with mood that is not daunted
by doubts whereby your perch, these hands, are haunted.

Agincourt to Verdun and Somme

At Agincourt, the chivalry of France
were slain with longbows by our yeomen stout,
who pinned them to their noble steeds to dance
a death-jig of astoundment with a shout,
surprised to find that earth's own salt had sting
enough to lop the spread from off the oak
of ancient peerage, bred to rule and bring
some modicum of culture to man's yoke.
How anguished must their women's wails have been
to see whole generations of that flower
of knighthood swept away, never again
to rule, to ride, to joust secure in power.
It was but foretaste of that later hell
in which *all Europe's* generations fell.

Permanently Dumb

I've seen the musk ox form a British square
(albeit it was round) to fend off jaws,
their calves protected in the middle there
by brandished adults' *horns*, rather than laws.
And now I've watched the stout cape buffalo
amass their numbers and assault a pride
of lions, rescue thus a calf—and throw
a lion overhead! (it surely died).
But in this civilized, this modern culture
in which I find myself, we're not allowed
horns to defend against a human vulture
or predator. Instead, we must act cowed,
call the authorities, and hope they come
before we're rendered permanently dumb.

Out of Kindness, Joy: A Moment in the Life of Dreon[*] the Brave

Bellowing warrior he, stout veteran
of many fights with towering, muscled slayers
from other, stranger outlooks than the one
he championed against Rome's proud purveyors.
A pagan to his death, he's never bowed
before a god who thinks himself alone
even in forests which old gods endowed
with holiness firm majesty has known.
And yet, confronted by one meagre child
who stepped in front of him to save her house
from being pillaged, he, no longer wild,
softened like Æsop's lion to the mouse
that gnawed the net through for him, as he bent
to comfort her from tears, his fury spent.

---

[*] nephew of Myrddin's patron, Gwenddoleu

My Toy Soldiers

I smuggled my toy soldiers past tall guards
who said that no *war-mongers'* toys could pass
their fearsome scrutiny; but my toy bards
explained to my toy army that their ass
was on the line, that they must sneak by quiet
and unobtrusive-like, else confiscated
be, their battles gone and only riot
remain, plopped in a box, uncelebrated.
So they crept by on tiny feet and brandished
their tiny weapons bravely, always ready
to go down fighting, faithful, never vanquished,
and even with all rope run out still steady.
Fortunately the guards were not expecting
they'd follow courses of their *own* electing.

The Mistress

She tolerated much, asserted little,
while he asserted much, and tolerated
only improvisations on the brittle
themes that his tongue imposed on her X-rated
companionship-for-hire. No courtesan
was she, simply a cushion for his ire,
an atmosphere that he might vent upon,
confusing anger for his inner fire.
Her life's become solidified, like clay
caught in an oven of imposing want
whose only purpose is to forge a way
to not relive a past that was too gaunt.
Hence she could never raise her gaze beyond
the encroaching wave to see it's but a pond.

Kitty Whispers to the Mutt

"Motley, your lack of enterprise is showing!
A lesson you should take from me: be active!
Explore! and see what prizes worth the knowing
are scattered hereabouts. You are the captive
of your complacency! *Disrupt* your rest
with *energy!* Are you not fed enough?
I hope this admonition feeds your *zest.*
If doubt still stills you, settle for a bluff!
What's out there is much better than what's here,
simply by *definition!* for this space
is limited, whereas it would appear
there's room enough beyond for us to race!
(I know you'd win, but still it would be fun—
you *know* that I'll be happy just to run!)"

Sphynx Cat

Is that a maze engraved upon your head?
or are you just constricting muscles there
in scowling at a thing some human said
that's not too flattering to one who's bare?
If it were not for that unique design,
I'd have to look at your uncomely face
and try to bypass thoughts of it and mine
some single trait of yours that has more grace.
And yet there is one, or so I've been told:
a marked propensity to snuggle close
and use your human to combat the cold,
seeming to offer love in overdose.
This trait would seem, I guess I should admit,
a charming even if well-practiced bit.

The Rhinoceros Slash Unicorn

Ancient accounts describe it to a tee
'Tis medieval legend that distorts
In body like a horse, the two agree
In poets' yarns, we almost hear its snorts
The great Pliny the Elder gives it feet
What folklore fancies slender, tufted hooves
That clop like those of elephants, not sleek
But notions follow stories' deep-set grooves
A stag-like head, as Strabo also states
Tapestries show a long and slender horn
A tail like what a boar incorporates
Delicate head in virgin's lap, forlorn
My head is with the ancients' strict description
My heart *prefers the fairytale's depiction*

What Name Should Pluto's Fourth Moon Bear?

A fourth moon? but I thought the experts felt
that Pluto was no planet: do *asteroids*
have moons? do ice balls in the Kuiper belt
have moons? Let experts mind their hemorrhoids
and leave astronomy to adults: pooh!
to all their silly Ph.D.s, if notions
devoid of sense can head-fake peer review
and wind up sailing academic oceans.
I say we name it 'Marble Number Four',
scientists having lost theirs long ago.
Give them the news: another we'll restore
in place of rocks in heads that claim to know.
How many must we find before these nuts
wake up and look beyond their group-think ruts!

Bad Hair Day

Long have I wished I might experience
a bad hair day, but try as might, no dice!
I go out in the drying wind and wince
to find that prospect one I can't entice.
I've shampooed up with too-great frequency,
to no avail, and shampooed not, but this
as well fell short: what *must I do* to see
my coiffure's disarray make things amiss?
I turned to medicine to find out why
my scalp's immune to such unpleasantness
no matter just how wet or just how dry
it gets from weather, my abuse, or stress:
it turns out that it helps, I'm now aware,
to have at least a modicum of hair.

Better Than Dull Soaps

Once tarred 'n' feathered for my dawning candor
with crayons when my elders held the cards,
stuck on a girl with gum—yes, I could stand 'er
while yet a lad—a love-life left in shards
by lipstick once I'd aged a bit, heart glued
to one who would've rather I'd been rich
and greased my hair back—which I tried once, shooed
away though I was then by bait 'n' switch—
and then by turns, by versifying pen's
and magic marker's rhyme, done in by thought
conforming not to what the lions' dens
decree we antelope must think, I've bought
some poetry-remover now, in hopes
it purges muses better than dull soaps.

Over and Above
[*Spenserian*]

Above this mass of soldier-words that march
in well-dressed ranks to meet reluctant ears
fly banners whose importance needs no starch
to soar, no gaudy hues allaying fears.
Their flags fade not, however many years
divide the setting down of weighty things
from when some yet unconquered mind appears
to pillage them and make them serve as wings.
For what's unchanged by life's recurrent flings
uplifts mind over that which does not last,
replacing it with truths whose meaning clings
to notions like results do to the past.
Such steps ring out unwearied, for they muster
to standards that will never lose their lustre.

Today's State Religion and Its Priests

The proud professors preach a hollow world
that has no Light within by which to think
and only atoms on the outside, twirled
particles globbed together in a sink
of energy that entropy will drink
the vital power from eventually,
so certain do they seem life's on the brink
of bless'd oblivion: a purpose-free
and pointless cosmos, unimpededly
dissolving, insubstantial, thoughtless, blind,
its irredeemable attempt to *be*
blocked by the absence of a saving mind.
Fools think our minds are fashioned by our heads!
and so their reason seldom leaves their beds.

Autumn Stream

Amongst the dense-packed growth of brush and alder,
a willow's fount rains withies towards a glazed
and whooshing sparkle, where leaves play Trafalgar
and ripples, slowed by shallowness, seem dazed.
It's here that salmon rest some from their crazed
and stubborn fight against the flow to bless
this course whose trail a brook's brave spirit blazed
to form the life's blood of a wilderness.
The human eye perceives a verdant mess!
but underneath, there's order, to sustain
its polyrhythmic pulse against duress
of the big beasts, and sun, and wind, and rain.
Here passage down and struggle upwards merge:
here downpour's depth meets love's primeval urge.

Christmas Day in Imagination

The wintry snow, which muffles sounds and makes
a calm hush of a Christmas morn, belies
rich color seen within, where time forsakes
the plain and drab to frame a child's surprise.
Our stream's broad bank, devoid of hazards, cries
its invitation on the wind to brave
each pallid drift of powdered snow that tries
its best to be inviting, like a cave.
Then marshmallow and cocoa start to crave
the mouths that will arrive, through windows seen,
whose eyes have noted smoke ascend to wave
and beckon chilly limbs to where the green
of ever-living boughs still guards the gifts
through which bold eagerness now coos and sifts.

Poetic Ecstasy
[Spenserian in 37 words]

Imagination circumvents surcease,
approximating serendipity,
intensifying temporal release,
eviscerating equanimity.
Equivocation's ambiguity
cerebrally awakens eloquence,
consigning surreptitious entropy
to categorical ebullience.
Corroborated by experience,
determination's irresistible
convictions mollify intelligence,
unwaveringly unimpeachable.
Illumination's plumb extemporizes,
awakens unexpected enterprises.

The War Within Myrddin Wyllt
[Spenserian 'Princess' Sonnet]

Mightily strove the tumult of his torn
worn cloak of thought that ought not blame its plight
right now on others' acts nor sink forlorn,
shorn of its fellows, into depths of night.
Worthy he'd surely be of kingship's height—
right worthy—were he only to ignore
more reasons than the wind and drop the fight
tight-wound about him by past fields of gore.
Gently would sister Gwyneth oft implore,
more softly than the wind, that he had spent
entirely all he owed to that great store
forlornly clung to in his lonely bent.
Quite firm his horror's grip upon the north;
blight meant he could not rule and bring peace forth.

Oddball
Sonnets

Let's Play Karma: I'm 'It'
[*Pushkin Sonnet*]

From outside, it appears a creature,
and yet it is aware: it lives
within said skin, an added feature,
a 'something else'—what waking gives.
Experience of pain or pleasure
will not its essence wholly measure,
for what it gets it wished once for—
for self, or someone else. Its store
of such recoilings, vast and heavy,
exists to admonish it what's right
and help it find its inner Light,
illuminator of the levy
that keeps the chaos sea without
so self can learn what self's about.

Selective Memory

I feel nostalgia for the stirring
of memories whose touch is kind,
the residue of acts unerring
whom no regrets have undermined.
To thinking neither numbed nor calloused,
they serve as anchor and as ballast
to firm the vessel lest it slip
from waves whose slopes might make it tip.
But other weights in the past's larder
are much less welcome when recalled,
occasions of which I'm appalled
that when remembered make life harder.
Selective memory is best
at never undermining zest.

Cheering the Parade
[*Keats Sonnet*]

How I have loved these wastes, this desert track
that feet have followed for some decades now
of reaching for the stars with every sigh,
trying to satisfy some unknown lack
that fails to yield its hold on my bruised brow,
this even though I know, here on my knoll,
there's nothing in this world except to die
makes fitting answer to the gnarled old knack
desire is born with in us: heart, endow
my mind the strength to stranglehold the lie
that life betrays when seeking to be whole
through things outside itself, whose warm appeal
offers illusions of a central role
for that which but parades as what is real.

Fountain of Song and Joy
[*Saraband Sonnet*]

That faith expands when circumstances
continue to be always good
belies the life that it enhances.
And one who's never braved the wood
knows only beds the soul may fall on
and not the strengths the soul must call on
if faced with strife where peace once stood.
It is the spirit of the chase—
peril's demand, the pull to climb
beyond one's mediocre place—
that is the spice that seasons time
and thrills us to our core, the well
that fills the thirst in struggle's spell—
songs' fount—which ease can only mime.

Emily
[*A Vaughanet*]

If pearl, onyx, and emerald adorn
her crown (and how dare I say otherwise),
then most would think it well-deserved when worn,
earned by the time-worn verse her heart devised.
But if words' *music* is perceived the measure,
may he be spared who would forego that treasure?
Perhaps her own appraisal of her worth
was true when she remarked the gems resembled
a flower that she owned: humble, the earth
applauds such modesty as makes men tremble.
For I sense that beneath her playful fawning
over some caller's gift, herself she saw
more accurately than the marquee awning
put up of late by those who stand in awe.

[*While not a* great *fan of her poetry, I do think hers a quite delightful mind!*]

Mind Out of Time
[Arabian Sonnet]

Unhitch this horse which pulls dead life along
where voice no longer follows in its throng
content to be the fading of a song
sung for a vanquished ear whose time was wrong.
Unharness what gives nostril to the air
(to sense the battle's flow) from crude despair
at dragging weight adorned not by the glare
of sun glancing on shield or sword-blade bare.
Bridle me up a worm, that time might see
the unrelenting tragic truth of me,
let loose upon an age that is not free.
Bridle a scarab to this ball of dung:
my only weapon is vain words I've flung
at fate's dull laughing face, to which they've clung.

A Proper Terza Rima Sonnet

I really don't know why I wrote this down
and must again be faced with the stark fact
it's hardly worth the spotlight of renown
but I remember times when every act
was magical: our door into a state
replete with charm, with every moment packed.
And there were others there who'd share that fate.
Clinging to curiosity like fools,
we'd soak up all the knowledge on our plate
to learn eventually that truths are tools
for prying open troubled thinking's gown
where hides her reasons and her precious jewels.
I really don't know why I wrote this down;
it's hardly worth the spotlight of renown.

A Reasonnet on Threefold Things

Important things arrange themselves in threes:
beginning, middle, end; or be it trees,
root-trunk-and-branch (branch bowing to life's breeze).
Or in the field of military knack,
advancing, standing ground, and going back,
all three maneuvers worth us keeping track.
Or happy, then indifferent, then sad,
which mark the moods with which we greet this mad
uncharted world: tearful, or calm, or glad.
The most important of all threefold ways
cuts time into what's fleeting, what lasts days
or years, and what's eternal, that which stays
unchanged and unaffected by time's flow,
only this last be'ng something one might know.

Monorhyme Fourteener on the Perenniality of Poetic Craft

The times they are a changin'; yet the human ear remains
and hears the self-same sounds it did when Buddha met the Jains.
It perks at sounds repeated and rejoices at refrains
so long as they're not sing-song or a stretch from meaning's lanes.
We still can stir with bold alliteration, like the Danes,
and use or *not* use end rime—there indeed we have made gains
in throwing off a yoke that choked off innovation's veins—
and yes, the thrill of homonyms and puns still twists our brains.
A poet's task is to extract thought's threads from tangled skeins
to weave a tapestry of sound the hearing mind retains:
the craft this unremunerated 'trade' involves in strains
of silence-tearing, boredom-slaying meaning still restrains
the flow of language by its careful shaping of the grains
of sand-scape into castles small yet mighty by its pains.

Note to Self

[Fourteener of fourteen 14-syllable sonnets]

Wit burns: it turns dull skies skull-wise
     and helps bland yelps gain mane.
Spat word, scattered, fought norm's sought forms,
     burst through worst, to mend blend.
Unless one guess which hat-stitch that
     lot was, what does pain gain?
Tease mem'ry's stem: think through link to
     reasons' seasons' end, friend.
Take time: make rime-patterns. That turns
     ears tow'rds tears, swords' sharp harp.
Fill page: *still* rage. Mold verse bold; terse.
     Seek ruts' bleak cuts: dig big.
Stilled, what spilled rot man is: ban his
     clipped crown, chipped-down 'smart' art!
Once-vile dunce-pile, lawn-fop on top:
     where's man's airs sans wig, dig?

Take me, shaky, back where knack dare
     rear head, tear-led sound found.
Bent knees sent trees skyward: fly, bird.
     Let gaze vet day's green scene.
Aid this jade kiss blown tow'rds known lords:
     praise gods' days, sod's round ground.
Grace, rise: face eyes' warm looks; storm brook's
     crossing, bossing (lean, mean).
O, for no more stress-borne mess: torn
     wings, *need* sings (freed) your cure.
Spun words run herds past fangs' last pangs
     (what, caged, got gauged pure lure).

Sestinas

Sestina After Dante

No longer am I ruled by shadow
here in love's unbecoming hills
ill-clothed by daylight's strawy grass
that dew once bathed in morning's green
now shadowed where night's standing stone
reminds eyes of the heart of woman.

The heart is hard *and* soft in woman
when caught by time's infernal shadow
hiding what crawls beneath the stone
that apes in miniature these hills
that lose their branches' gown of green
to languor in the golden grass.

Now all that grows here *is* this grass
once trod by footfalls of a woman
whose golden locks outcurl the green
of mem'ry and outshine the shadow
cast by these obelisks whose hills
have crumbled from once solid stone.

The only relic here is stone,
in contrast to the untrod grass
surrounding what once passed these hills
to find that vale that once was woman
before it fell to fallow shadow
attempting to return to green.

For only life can claim the green
belied by hills and path and stone
that now yield only wake of shadow
whose cool encourages the grass
to rise beneath the heel of woman
like serpents hiding in their hills.

And yet deep comfort are these hills
that hold the memory of green,
if not the truth of it (a woman
that's made of something less than stone
in hardness) for this flattened grass
reveals there's gold beneath the shadow.

Though brunt of hills be carven stone,
their skin may green, should thirsting grass
be trod by woman, not just shadow.

While Great Suns Set
[*Trimeter Sestina*]

I saw some people pause
to watch the great sun set
beyond the sea's horizon,
a portion of its face
still clinging to this world
till after I drove past.

And thinking of the past,
this image gave me pause,
wondering if the *world*
will be the thing that's set
before too long, its face
hid by my *mind's* horizon.

When young, one's own horizon
is something to get *past*
until you find that face

that always gives you pause,
into which you may set
as if it *were* the world

and you the sun. That world
becomes the mind's horizon
beyond which most will set,
to blend in with the past,
but at which one will pause
and never hide her face.

I find it hard to face
the changes in this world,
wishing there'd be a pause
at some well-marked horizon
that it could not get past
until my sun had set.

Yet with my mind's eye set
upon that one fair face
whose form defines the past
for me, I face the world
renewed, and the horizon
within me's where I pause,

horizon where that face—
the *world* to me, once passed—
gives pause as great suns set.

The Human Condition According to Alchemy
[*Quasi-Sestina*]

Life is the vestibule of tombs.
The land where thoughts reside is parched.
O what a sorry thing is man,
who compasses all types of soils,
some needing, some eschewing rain,
all shunning wisdom's chill embrace.

Mirages are what lusts embrace.
What even love aspires to, tombs
will always interrupt, warm rain
its substance. (To decide that parched
is better soils both wit and man.)

Yes, it is such a course that man,
though puzzled by it, must embrace,
where tested soils become his tombs,
his tongue parched in the pouring rain.

For it is tears that rain in man.
For that is what the parched embrace
to scour out tombs in hardened soils.

Lust soils the rain that carves our tombs.
And what man can't embrace stays parched.

Parched soils embrace the rain, as man his tombs.

The Dividend of Controlling How One Thinks
[*Tritina*]

The taste of expectations' wine is bitter
when self-made victims find that they have grown
a culture on their slide that smothers cheer.

No better off are they that chase their cheer,
for when they find it not, their minds turn bitter,
a poutiness that shows they're not yet grown.

Both courses have I followed, and the groan
that plagued my inner voice was like a cheer
saluting what was best at making bitter.

But bitter now has grown into good cheer.

Rondeaux, Roundels, etc.

What I Told the Trees
[*Rondeau*]

I told the trees to speak their mind,
tell how it felt to be confined
within strict limits man has made,
this concrete desert spawned of jade
whose green's a sickly patchwork rind.

But they see me as dense and blind,
since what they sprout has been consigned
the space above my head—for shade!
     I told the trees.

The great ones leave *my* thoughts behind!
for they on centuries have dined,
while I through each day's threats must wade
newly disheartened or dismayed:
I feel a kinship with your kind,
     I told the trees.

Folksong Rondeau: Concerning the Moon Tonight

The unadorned truth oft I spy,
the play of light on cold blue sky—
the moon hiding behind a cloud
pretending it to be a shroud
then hopping out, all glib and sly.

Nature don't even have to try!
she does it simply 'on the fly',
no orders given said out loud—
       the unadorned truth.

With other truths I sometimes vie,
and some are true, I won't deny,
but they're adorned, or sown and plowed,
and spoken for or disavowed:
all mine gets is a heartfelt sigh,
       the unadorned truth.

A Timely Hint
[Rondeau Redoublé]

A timely hint of disarray
that warns the day is poorly spent
will be what afternoon will say
to whose wrong way the morning's sent.

In flush of youth I did my stint
at being bold and bright and gay
but didn't always make the rent—
a timely hint of disarray!

Yet onward pressed the poise of play
that gave to life its shallow bent
hiding noon's deeper shade of grey
that warns the day is poorly spent.

And thus I failed to heed the glint—
gold scribbling on my walls of clay—
belying what is set in print
will be what afternoon will say.

Those orders one cannot belay
that have already made their dent
direct what afternoon must pay
to whose wrong way the morning's sent.

So who at the beginning went
for what results in vain display
may later lack a sturdy tent
and not much like what's on life's tray:
        a timely hint.

Where Scholars Play
[*Roundel*]

Where scholars *play*, the brave mind *toils*:
it digs a deeper truth that way,
whose measure is the souls it roils
        where scholars play.

No academia delay
can rob of worth such inroads' spoils,
for they're the dawn of light and day.

They're brave who sow and dare the coils
of fixed opinion: half-baked clay
can crack—there should be better soils
        where scholars play.

Rondel on the New National Bird

It was not clear the last time round
the ostrich had become our bird,
head buried so that what is heard
is all controlled from underground.

No light may enter: only sound,
which makes its fix on life absurd.
It was not clear the last time round
the ostrich had become our bird.

Our far-off past, it seems, had found
a better wingèd one, inferred
by many now to be interred
beneath the earth (with no raised mound).
It was not clear the last time round
the ostrich had become our bird.

Rondine? What the hell is a Rondine?

So many forms, so little time:
am I to leave some unengaged?
leave unresolved this war I've waged
to master every way that slime
might yet be forced into a rhyme?
And now another's has me gauged—
        so many forms!

It seems I'm forced again to chime
in on what has me unenraged
to be constricted, cabined, caged
till voice has finished with its crime—
        so many forms.

Villanelles

Would-Be Pastorale

To nature's reach would I my talents turn
and sing of man in verdure's bosom held:
I look, but see a setting stark and stern.

Inspired by brown of trunk and green of fern,
eyes are uplifted and the mind compelled—
to nature's reach would I my talents turn!

But power wires intrude, my eyes soon learn,
and trees I once had seen have now been felled:
I look, but see a setting stark and stern.

I long for streams; for woods my senses burn,
for tangled brush, for groves not cursed but spelled—
to nature's reach would I my talents turn.

But scent of acrid gases fuels concern
with din of metal horse and wheels' screech yelled:
I look, but see a setting stark and stern.

So far it's been my destiny to yearn
for chirping air yet mostly find it quelled.
To nature's reach would I my talents turn:
I look, and see a setting stark and stern.

That Yet Would Leave You Whole

There is no strong device I might employ
to twist you to my way of seeing things
that yet would leave you whole and not my toy.

I've tried gentle persuasion, to annoy
that part of you insistently that sings
there is no strong device I might employ

that you would not see through and re-alloy.
A gaping dearth of tools brave cunning brings
that yet would leave you whole and not my toy.

The sorcery of poetry, my joy,
can bend you yet not turn you from your stings:
there is no strong device I might employ

that could do that, and thus am I left coy
and hesitant when care's insistence rings
that yet would leave you whole and not my toy.

So tell us, luv, what sly approach or ploy
might serve to soften pebbles your pride slings?
There is no strong device I might employ
that yet would leave you whole and not my toy.

Villanelle of a Once-Shy Dancer or Hanging Man

I never thought I'd live to see the day
that from the limelight of the earth's decor
my head should be plucked forth to twist this way.

For once, the reasons all stack up and weigh
impressive measures as they seek the floor—
I never thought I'd live to see the day—

yet there is nothing lessened from dismay
the lesson of this step would not restore:
my head *should* be plucked forth to twist this way.

While body effervesces, prone to stray,
inertia's faith gives way to what's in store—
I never thought I'd live to see the day

the consequences would out-jolt the play
brought forth by consequence: it's just the *score*
my head should be plucked forth to twist this way.

Have I become the air's bauble to sway?
I know I've never danced like this before.
I never thought I'd live to see the day
my head should be plucked forth to twist this way.

Life's Petals

Life's petals, now, are parting cloaks
Unveiling promise in the glare
That makes them wilt beneath the oaks.

The oak-king's sacrifice provokes
Surprise at his unworried air:
Life's petals, now, are parting cloaks.

For once the rain of April soaks
The plants, of what must they beware
That makes them wilt beneath the oaks?

It can't be wary thoughts which coax
Their secrets from them, aims they bare—
Life's petals, now, are parting cloaks!

So could it just be nature's hoax,
Born of our overheated stare,
That makes them wilt beneath the oaks?

Too full a touch of sunlight's strokes
And youth's glow fades where flowers dare.
Life's petals, now, are parting cloaks:
That makes them wilt beneath the oaks.

The Loss of the Merry Villanelle

This form I once had relish for,
that tempted me to try my hand,
has now become a thing of yore.

For villanelles have closed the door
on my imagination—canned,
this form I once had relish for!

This pattern which makes mind's ear sore
from repetition's cold demand
has now become a thing of yore.

I do lament the loss, my score
now minus one—one once thought grand!
this form I once had relish for.

But my attempt to mold life's roar
into its shape and not sound bland
has now become a thing of yore.

What forms are left that do not bore
will have to do, for as things stand
this form I once had relish for
has now become a thing of yore.

Other Forms Involving Refrain

Whom I Only See in Dreams
[Triolet]

Let's dance a two-step in the night,
my love, for the break of dawn looms
closer with every kiss we fight.
Let's dance a two-step in the night,
pretending absence is a blight
imposed on others in cramped rooms.
Let's dance a two-step in the night,
my love, for the break of dawn looms.

Triolet for the Lost

How sad this generation's wise
that what surrounds it stands for naught.
Nihilists now define the prize:
how sad this generation's wise.
Sensation thrills and blinds most eyes:
once found, it's not known what was sought.
How sad this generation's wise
that what surrounds it stands for naught.

Where I Wished to Wend
[Swinburne's Octain Refrain]

Disoriented sweetly
from where I wished to wend,
my sense of independence
dissolves into transcendence
when you and I discreetly
join forces in a blend,
disoriented sweetly
from where I wished to wend.

Right Sweet and Left with Naught
[Three Madrigals]

I.

Right sweet it was to fall into your trap,
Sweet to be captured by your ambuscade
And learn of love before I learned of jade.

I woke, awakened by a gentle slap,
My new possession not subject to trade.
Right sweet it was to fall into your trap,
Sweet to be captured by your ambuscade.

Experience of you became the map
That helped me find the way back to your glade
To rest from life's pale glare beneath your shade.
Right sweet it was to fall into your trap,
Sweet to be captured by your ambuscade
And learn of love before I learned of jade.

II.

Vain course of years, all thoughts of you suppressed,
The warm regard untampered-with and strong,
How when I reawakened heart did long!

Time's passages imposed a sort of test
Of whether I would recognize your song:
Vain course of years, all thoughts of you suppressed,
The warm regard untampered-with and strong.

When sight of where our lips had often pressed
Stir memories, it's like a ringing gong,
Insistent passion trampling right and wrong.
Vain course of years, all thoughts of you suppressed,
The warm regard untampered-with and strong,
How when I reawakened heart did long!

III.

A warmth once felt for me returned the while:
It held the harmony my singing sought,
But then it cooled and I am left with naught.

Time's agony of want became a smile
Of pleasure over what the years had wrought.
A warmth once felt for me returned the while:
It held the harmony my singing sought.

But saved from jade, my heart knew not that guile
By which most hearts hold onto what life's bought.
My love, unchanged, by that same snare was caught!
A warmth once felt for me returned the while:
It held the harmony my singing sought,
But then it cooled, and I am left with naught.

Life's Lesson
[Kyrielle]

Youth's spirit grasps the life it rides
with both hands clutching at its mane:
the now is strong, and what abides
must wait until youth's powers wane.

183

One's prime is poised to kick life's sides
and spur it on to come-what-may:
the now is strong, and what abides
can always wait another day.

When storms brew and the shifting tides
of fortune need much seeing to,
the now is strong, and what abides
can hold off while we muddle through.

And in the trough whose 'calm' divides
last wave from next, when rest is sought,
the now is strong, and what abides
gets banished once again to thought.

So then when age at last collides
with what's been wrought to be life's fate,
the now is strong, and what abides
is what is left upon one's plate.

Wave to Wave, Lake to Lake
[*Trijan Refrain*]

The soul that I am closest to
is far away and hears
no lookout's notice of the due
course of this life, which steers
nearer to her each turn it makes
tacking across these mirror lakes
  nearer to her,
  nearer to her
however many shores it takes.

The soul that I am closest to
has a good life: her own.
The treasures in my hold are few,
fit for just one, alone

upon these waves, whose deep troughs hide
the masts and sails I raise inside
      upon these waves,
      upon these waves
through which my faery sloop must glide.

The soul that I am closest to,
unwitting, holds the wheel
from far off: keeps its bearing true
in ways that loom most real
to eyes that see beyond the mist
dividing lakes my need has kissed,
      to eyes that see—
      two eyes that see—
beyond the portage to the tryst.

The Spirit of Asserting Reason First
[*Chant Royal*]

I never vote unless I have, in file,
an army at my back, with which to chase
entrenched corruptness off to join the pile
of failures past, in order to replace
the fabric of it with a better story
derived from history's la*bor*atory
of tried and tested means of mending bone
and flesh of governments, whose forms are prone
to swell in power till we are immersed
in rules whose purpose is to turn to stone
the spirit of asserting reason first.

The character of government is vile
the best of times, its greed for power base
and treacherous, ready to take a mile
per inch it's given in its stormy race
against the individual, whose dory
for fleeing such a ship is dilatory,
from natural reluctance to be shown

an *unenthusiastic* subject drone,
one whose obedience is interspersed
with serious attempts to train or hone
the spirit of asserting reason first.

No autocratic pharaoh of the Nile
competed with today in weight of mace
for beating down the object of his bile,
nor had he a computer interface
for tracking down each detailed category
of unchecked box—whether by Whig or Tory—
that could be indication mind has flown
the coop of those who still obey the throne
in all respects, the way it was rehearsed
in *rulers'* minds—whose ministers bemoan
the spirit of asserting reason first.

It seems no exercise of wit or guile
can bend the destiny we humans face,
the crashing waves of 'Comrade!' or 'Sieg heil!'
that interrupt the vital, normal pace
of commerce or of getting amatory
with fellow souls with whom we share this lorry
spiriting us through times that are the clone
of other times in which the crop was sown
that springs up now around us in a burst
of retribution for our having *blown*
the spirit of asserting reason first.

And yet there is a path of word and wile
which (followed) leads to *slow-decaying* grace
of governance: we followed it a while
(it's called the Constitution). Yet embrace
its literal intent today and gory
will be your end, since state's confiscatory
taxation, waste, and hubris so has grown
as blurs the lines of what remains one's own
and that for which one can't get reimbursed,
namely nostalgia for once having known
the spirit of asserting reason first.

And even though I know I'm not alone
in wishing we could reinstate the tone
of healthy fear of government, the worst
has happened: one can't reach—even by phone—
the spirit of asserting reason first.

When the Time Comes
[*Quatern*]

When the time comes and the sky falls,
will men recall the wavering
that led to it? Forgetful calls
betray Cassandra's voiceless sting.

Prophetess, will your voice still ring
when the time comes and the sky falls?
Can ears retain what prophets sing
amidst the tunes at shopping malls?

Do people care that their high walls
block sight as well as suffering?
When the time comes and the sky falls,
they'll see what walls are harboring.

But I refuse to wait to bring
this truth forth: my discretion stalls
to grasp the upshot that will cling
when the time comes and the sky falls.

A Quatern on the Moon's Constancy

Fitting the moon in my small boat
requires its silver be condensed
in weight and compass till it float
on silvered tongue, whose song commenced

when first I felt the Queen of Night
fitting the moon in my small boat
of verse and sighs with her soft might.
But lately her reflection's coat

appears to me across a moat
of tears purposes foiled have made.
Fitting the moon in my small boat
seems just as fitting as I fade

as in the pristine sheen of youth's
esprit. Such beauty does not gloat:
its constancy's the *cause* of truth's
fitting the moon in my small boat.

Do the Dixon
[Does not involve refrain, but I stuffed it in here anyway]

Okay, I'll bite. The labor
requires I lodge a neighbor
    out past the last sound stressed
of much less weight emphatic
than what it forms the attic
    or basement of, once dressed.

Two female rhymes to start with,
a male to ply the heart with,
    then one more pair of femmes,
these followed by a male one—
but do not use a stale one,
    your lines will not be gems!

I think I might just manage
within my own life-spannage
      if slant rhyme be allowed:
I'll cap the ultra-feminine
with like effect made eminent,
      refusing to be cowed.

In setting forth intrepid,
avoiding what is tepid,
      I now declare a truce
upon that other gender
than mine—the one that's tender
      and subject to abuse.

To show I'm being serious,
let tongue become imperious
      and go where it will go!
The critics will be furious
and brand my notions spurious—
      who cares: it's all for show.

The Makings of the Sage
[*Monchielle*]

How did this monstrous gloom
sneak up behind our backs
and compass us about?
Does not intention's aim
retain its ancient clout?

How did this monstrous gloom
enclose our world and leave
so little light in eyes
oft closed, rarely opened,
and from disuse unwise?

How did this monstrous gloom
come to be thought normal

and not a punishment?
Is it not obvious
it's of demonic bent?

How did this monstrous gloom
enchain man's loyalties
inside its gilded cage?
It's knowing we're not free
distinguishes the sage.

Pooky

[*Monotetra*]

A Siamese was Pooky, full
of personality and bull
along with sparsity of wool—
     memorable, memorable.

One time he jumped down from the roof
and then up on the car's hood—poof!
through windshield, looked at us in spoof:
     never aloof, never aloof.

And when I'd write a poem, paw
would meddle with the pen it saw
a-weaving back and forth, to gnaw
     at my heart's awe, at my heart's awe.

Too quickly did he canter on
to where all great felines have gone
when they no longer man the lawn:
     to Avalon, to Avalon.

Traditional Irish Measures

Tarry
[*Rannaigheacht Bheag*]

Tarry long, maid of mindful
song, to ferry heart's handle
across chasms egged idle
by prideful thought's ebbed angle.

Graze, eyes once held, now hidden,
jelled glib in ways of women.
Cradle softly spun silken
tongue's lilt in lofty linen.

Faith, test life's likely limits:
crave zest, like feisty ferrets.
Buttress weal with spruced spirits'
boost brought near its means' merits.

Prime the scene for charm's cheeky
ways—arms that preen don't parry.
Clasp a tone that's bold, breezy,
grown easy, tasked to tarry.

Faraway Voice
[Óglachas of Rannaigheacht Bheag]

Softness of mouth and manner
housed in her breathless banter
makes my lonely pulse patter
with ache its only answer.

Another's warm hearth harbors
her loved form—art *my* ardor,
rift-born thoughts my angst's arbor:
trees' star-wrought gift I garner.

Empty air's roar is raucous:
wind pairs her with poor plaudits.
Storm's choice uplifts what's lauded:
warmth's voice that sifts through softness.

Play, O Flute of Spring
[Rionnard]

Aftermath of measure,
mend pleasure's path quaintly.
Let each finger firmly
linger, fretting faintly.

Lift winter's spent spirits,
spark lent by swift swallow.
Steady man's moods: mellow
the wood's heady hollow.

Spring shifts to bright banter.
Bold gift, your light leisure.
Make laughter last: linger,
aftermath of measure.

To a Soldier
[*Lethrannaegecht Mor*]

Hail, warrior, well met:
far a fellow that!
Brave, lingers in light—
one bright core of cat!

It's lucky for us
we lack not such souls
amongst our number
to stir when wrath rolls.

Were we all peaceniks,
where's war's wherewithal?
We'd soon be but slaves
or graves—you're our wall!

Best for the whole world
you haul ass war-wise.
You're out for them too,
see life through their eyes.

You're *made* of the world's
muddy boots, you bet!
Therefore all the more:
hail warrior, well met.

Age's Edge
[*Casbairdne*]

Age's edge, dregs detected,
aids course where tread's untested.
Still, with its call clandestine,
some fall, with catch requested.

Experience suspended,
fear leaves past tense untempted.

With old wrath's ties untended,
the wise path lies preempted.

Strife's essence gets invested
in stress, life's jest rejected.
Ledge that's safe, sage, ancestral?
age's edge, dregs detected.

"They just wouldn't stay still!"
[*Casbhairn (old school)*]

Mortimer the mortician,
Bored, became a beautician.
Soon, scared by his scrutiny,
Dared many to mutiny.

Where others might mollify,
He didn't quite qualify.
Hence he served them certainer:
Murdered them did Mortimer.

Lone I Thrive
[*Rannaigheacht Ghairid*]

Lone I thrive
and won't just take a swan dive
like a boat that needs a fleet
social sheep hemmed by the hive

Inner thrills
mean my thinner throng fulfills
by meek design's deft desire
my warm fire outshines their frills

My thoughts probe
from undistracted brain lobe

deep mysteries that resist
minds still kissed by taming's toad.

None will groan
when I pay back this starred stone,
yet I'll have gained more than they
in the way that we're *all* 'lone'.

Got Too High

Dad makes wings,
gives me two of the damned things,
but then it gets out of hand:
when I land short, guess who sings!

Gods, who lurk,
put the fat lady to work,
her song bringing to an end
your old friend me, a real jerk.

By wing'd cape
two of us try to escape
from Crete: sun's heat unwaxed me,
and the sea was there to gape.

Cast no blame,
though, on dad: mine is the shame.
Must've gotten way too high
for men to fly—down I came!

Don't be sad:
you see, not even I'm mad
since I'm mourned by three nice girls
wearing only curls—plus dad.

L o n g . . .

in compost,
part of what I am is toast,
not much use in soil's rebirth
and not worth what it once grossed.

Lacking bread,
my voice gums bold words instead;
seeking purchase on the wind,
these rescind what storms have said.

Toothless song,
transmelodious and wrong
for some, still it preserves rich
ash for which the day's wastes long.

Pferyllt's Prayer

azure rain
sullies blue sky's cloudless lane
the sun's clearness tensely tinged
lest light's glow impinge on pain

blackened breeze
inkblot out all but the knees
I'm brought to by regret's path
wrath of the past's travesties

pink child-soul
deemed dewy fresh yet a toll
old lives' woe will weigh it down
as its thorn's crown and a shoal

good red road
that leads beyond yearning's goad
point purposes for the best
where light's quest is truth's abode

silver wheel
projecting what was deemed real
that made the inner realm loom
adorn doom with your appeal

softest gold
strewn on ground that's growing cold
put poultice to the bard's voice
let words' choice be visions bold

silver grain
whose spark of light means my gain
sprout the rays that comprehend
and transcend this azure rain

Morning Dew

Morning dew
dawns adorning thoughts of you
that night has left, leaving lots
of grieving spots bright in hue.

Drink up, air,
that which sun will shrink, not share,
one sparkling moment, no more,
show meant to adore and dare.

The sun yawns
over feelings flung on lawns
by light's storming of love's lair
there where the morning dew dawns.

Darkness Came to Fast
[Rannaigheacht Mhor (óglachas)]

Darkness came to fast, not feast,
mane of beast life's partied past.
Ask the barely tempted trees:
in air's emptied breeze they bask.

Ought I opt, like them, to shade
those made lost by sight of sky?
Whiles my highest boughs risk rays
of now's daze, eyes' unseen isle.

Light eats the dark it daubs, face
like smart snobs caught in base beats.
It greased past in spark-less shame:
darkness came to fast, not feast.

What the Sea Sings
[Rannaigheacht Mhor]

The sea sings and strums the sand[']s[,]
shifting needs beneath our feet—
still to it, *moving* to man's
soothing jams, whose swill is sweet.

Intoxicating tones tempt,
approximating meant modes.
Yet they fall short, their lure lent
to abort—*cure*—our kempt codes.

We rest far too sure fate shares
our best goals, then mar the means.
Plotting outshouts ocean's airs,
squares not with what the sea sings.

Three Ears the Cat

Three Ears I call her: that cat
fears naught that walks and wields claws.
A scrapper! wee runt that ran
free once of mankind's lax laws.

Being pushed—unstably stashed—
between masters made her pace.
Soon on out of doors she'd dash,
be rash for more room to race.

Leonidas needles her
fierce pride to wax stern in strife.
When her ear got split it spurred
word of thanks she lit my life.

Sad it is I lived too lean
with her need for new digs back.
All felt her fur melt for me;
Three Ears I call her, that cat.

Fire

Fire has filtered out the dross,
delivered life from ruts' chains,
prideful things lost that held hopes
inside the moats of old aims.

I'm hollowed out; I ache; still
there's space now for a new call.
Satisfaction's gone, a gift
to dawn's sifted ash, that's all.

Gratification's gap greets
the past's gaze: cold lies its lyre.
To serve others is now's need,
greed smothered to free love's fire.

Raven of War

Clean earth's heft of brittle bones,
the little left of worth's yield.
Through death's still no reason roams:
a season's groans fill yon field.

Feast, raven of war: the wind,
craven, has teased its sore scent,
aftermath of a dire din
where ire and wrath, to win, went.

Feats have filled cold halls with loss
to greet what skilled skalds have sung.
Hungry pecks toothlessly toss
sundry necks ruthlessly wrung.

Nibbling need has brought sky's best:
not your league, those sibling crows!
Raven, whittle lean what's left.
Clean earth's heft of brittle bones.

Expectant Silence
[*Deibhidhe*]

Wilting quiet, quill-less, dulls.
Unstinting stillness stifles:
words well in one's gut, their gift
quelled. Birds mutter a makeshift.

Waste it seems. Yet searing sound
gleams with haste, hearing's background.
Calm's flurry, which breezes bring,
eases qualms, worry wilting.

Deft Is the Dragon

Dragon, dimmed is your gaunt glow
that haunts simmering sorrow.
You I talk of some would slay
for blocking hope's new highway.

Old the truths your talons guard,
value that skirts the schoolyard.
Fearful of what's tried and true,
wide most veer from your venue.

Wake, ways of old: breathe forth fire!
Boldly brave man's warped empire.
Fools see in your death new dawn,
view night in your breath's beacon.

Dark, deliver stars, light's lure,
giver of sight its censure.
Why discard ways that have won:
day's hard, and deft the dragon.

Vision Song

Littlefeather am I, old
tether truth cannot cuckold.
Guide-beasts bound to ends of ills
sound feasts' impending perils.

I, well-anchored to known knolls,
hanker not to roam rat-holes.
To turn timid runs great risks:
soul's journey takes no tourists.

Heart picks the path that's purest:
marvels make it picturesque.
Need—my knife, aged, all-weather—
carves life. *Lead*, Littlefeather!

Deibhidhe in 'Beat' Mode[*]

Me, I'm at heart a hippy:
I thrust art at entropy.
The withered past I pity:
what lasts gives it gravity.

On flow'rs I feast, yet with swords'
pow'rs at least latent recourse.
The wise all revere valor,
else fear the tall traveler.

Acid, wine, women, and song,
that's quite fine for a furlong.
Time darted past, fierce and free:
me, I'm at heart a hippy.

Where Have All the Flower Children Gone
[*Séadna*]

So, the song-wrights pale. A plastic
image of themselves they sell.
My how pollen's flowers' faded
towers, tall an' jaded, jell!

Your glories once displayed splendor's
worth as nascent inner ore,
mined extract—the selfless, savored
kindness man was flavored for.

Rouse from sleep the slumb'ring model's
ultra-meek yet thund'ring throng.
Moments are love's only ova:
doff the gloves and sow the song!

---

[*] This and the previous poem observe the rule called *rinn*, where each couplet's second end-word has one more syllable than its first.

Elegy

Youth once gaped as a great rebirth
stirred man's brute to brave love's limb.
I can still hear song's fair flowers
fill the air to bower's brim.

Spryly we spilled our loves' delight!
Night and day, we tilled our times
till laws phased out love with limits—
today's hardly mimics mine.

Music's light now lurks in corners,
pervasive dearth in night's knell.
Still in life's librettos, lyrics'
echoes fulfill spirits' spell.

What the flower child held holy
eludes now, wild sport of spoof.
Memory strives but trails, turning
to wives' tales my yearning youth.

Séadna on the Photo of a Nebula

Curling clouds composed of plasma
amass, each a nub of night.
Into filaments it's twisted:
must this still resist our sight?

Teachers, hiding haste in ivied
vaults, refrain from facing facts.
Groundless myths of mass they're bawling:
wisdom gives these all the axe!

Carefully constructed theory
reasons *current* rules our roof:
magnetic swirls, stars entraining—
yet why paint so plain a proof?

For few lecturers are looking;
care they'd need to notice night.
Gravity can't cause such patterns
by *its* laws, nor lanterns light.

Methinks the thimpletons command,
whose minds' blinds are shrinking shrouds,
else explain why those up early
cannot see the curling clouds.

Craft's Cunning

Cunning, craft show useful yearnings
nest in every ear that hears.
Similar sounds, fast and frequent,
cast words so their sequence sears.

End-rhyme alone—that old sawhorse,
the has-been—is a cracked crutch.
More is needed to mold meaning
ere ear heed its keening clutch.

Alliteration stands steadfast:
far forebears leaned on its lilt.
And consonance remains manly,
song's enhanced, uncanny quilt.

Most internal rhyme is timely:
it leers almost beneath note.
And grammar, graced with tense talents,
traced, will make a balanced boat.

With all aboard, gall's great gunboat
bulges with force, fore and aft!
All await *un*silent running's
tall traits of a cunning craft.

Two-Way Telekinesis

This morning's signs seem to whisper
surprising dreams dipped and sauced.
Promises of sun soon sever
gloom, with torrent's lever lost.

Yet even had that crude crowbar
marred it, mood would match it not.
Deep within, I burst out brightened,
spin my own much lightened lot.

How could the sky *fail* to follow
so hale a fellow's beamed bliss!
Storm's spit is a waning wonder:
bit of *inner* thunder this.

The Nickname 'Sordid Sage'
[*Droighneach (óglachas)*]

Satisfies the surreal. Tall, it tubes me sparingly.
It's what's staring me in the fierce face of solitude.
My Attic attitude it compasses caringly
while wearing me to the ball like a perched platitude.

Sordid implies outer, a touch terrible:
what dare live all to the hilt defies fathoming.
Sage suggests inner stations, to which wherewithal
adjusts to information's guarded gathering.

Sordid Sage sort o' sizes it up, calibrates
a wide base for the caliphate it fortifies.
The term might stick, like a hat size; for it celebrates
what elevates the bitter sap that satisfies.

Hawthorn Blossoms

In scent's subtle edge, in splendor bright and beautiful
on hedge or bush, tenderness acts as overlay
disguising hard young spikes dire and dutiful
that stand as brutal guardians of the everyday.

Like a light dusting of snow, many miniscule
five-petaled spots of white glow thrust forth, threatening
a return to cold from summer's varied vestibule
of bold hues thrumming with warmth's ribald reckoning.

But fear not: exuded pollen, the soft anti-snow,
eludes eyes as it lifts life aloft to copulate
with bloom. Clipped bouquets of may face their vertigo
up where maypoles play (whose place we populate).

Your pale purity blocks the way, prevents invasion:
from sensual to demur, your mask is mutable.
Dense spears double the might of your sweet persuasion
in scent's subtle edge, in splendor bright and beautiful.

Law's Purpose
[*Droighneach (old school)*]

Limiting the size and scope granted government
underwent mimicking ere it finely fermented
into lip-service alone, that half abhorrent
torrent that rings a bit nervous, its truths tormented.

I'm wise to the wiles of the savvy sultanate's
horizon-grabbing gulp in its fit of annexing
that which it can't produce itself: it's the ultimate
cult 'n' it fears we'll reduce it by law's limiting.

The Local Faust Was First a Priest

I wuz livin' on limited resources,
driven by fate's G-forces ta seek sorcery.
I'd been where art exits, where gaiety disgorges.
(The laity jus' forges on, gets on gorgeously.)

Thought I might dump it (me vows) ta find verity
in a strumpet—teased terribly to dare ickiness!
O great whiskey flask upstairs, it's empathy
we ask o' thy sympathy o' lent loveliness!

Still, the ground struggle ekes on, the ultimate
bubble, cult in a cat's eye, many-minuted.
Poverty: with 'im long an' ya edge tow'rds intimate.
Intricate, with what I wuz livin' on limited.

The Divil's Charm

It's the divil yer will's wonderin' concernin'?
This from some sermon's thunderin' thought-train terminus?
As a spirit, it suffices he act unnervin'—
some myrrh, then, or enough ice as woos worthiness.

For heat's his thing, flame's fiery lustiness,
which sin's priory, crustiness, fakes finessin'.
Only stamina can withstand stuffiness,
one's anima a scruffy mess from dire duressin'.

Is this Scratch's innate charm? Light's lackluster
*dis*patches from thought's hat muster bright blusterin'!
Sumps often swivel, lest those thereunder
dare hunger; it's the divil: yer will's *wanderin'*.

Limo Driver Knows His Place But Finds It Odd

Duty's deference demonstrates enterprise,
a reference to what temper tries that's surprising
yet needed if this fellow is to fraternize,
be mellow, and not satirize unsound surmising.

Greeks with learning served crude Rome: no deft dissenter
let this enter in between earning and temperance.
For though I be a roaring underground aquifer,
the lot prefer thunder drowned in duty's deference.

After Plato

Certainty of opinion: the mad mandolin
of lectures; grand omen of dust's dominion.
Where's your belated sting, o daft daffodil
that cremated math-mobile airs in curt cotillion?

All that's ever known are matters eternal,
wee kernel within tatters of time's tournaments.
Things worldly can change: doubts determine
that they return unearned regard with *play* permanence.

Let mind wax empirical, to enrapture
then capture the meant miracle: being accurate.
To be too sure means dancing with disaster,
this after enhancing things angry and aspirate.

A special risk is the unanswered and internal:
infernal or celestial, it will throb thermally
till some self-unctuous air opt to uncurtain
some burden half seen, but in sumptuous certainty.

[*See also page 120*]

Traditional Welsh Measures

Key: [(c)] means *with cynghanedd* (strict rules required of Welsh bards)

Far-Off Love
[*Englyn Milwr*]

Treat well the ones you soften
and think on me not often
but well, o pool I quaff in.

Justice [*(c)*]

Justice, the dirk, jousts with dark,
whose lanced means has lost a mark
in life's store, its new laugh stark.

Cute Cruelty [*(c)*]

Eyes ask sweetly; nose seeks tail;
she purrs soft, a show: prize sale!
With man so fooled, the mice flail.

Song of the Wolf
[*Englyn Penfyr*]

You hound us, man, because we share *your* taste,
will eat in haste what you, there,
might hoard, because we wolves dare.

We ignore fixed boundaries *you* impose,
borders that you chose to please
a life centered around ease.

You stay in place most of your year, while we
run free, seeking the wild deer
or lesser game without fear.

We dread no creature but you, whom we grant
your space, since scant game wends through
lands that have seen what you do.

But herds you keep attract our paws, since game
is all the same: it lures jaws
of those that know not man's laws.

But know this, man: we do not seek *your* flesh
to enmesh in teeth, for meek
though your young be, you all reek!

You smell of predator, not prey, and we
learned to flee from your warm way
of guns and wolf-traps that say:

"You may not share with us this earth, our home,
which you roam: when pressed by dearth
of game, give man a wide berth!"

No Rest for the Wicked
[*Awdl Gywydd*]

All mankind does frailly mends
askew ends, wild since childbirth.
Therefore, one strikes ore who asks
that our tasks teach us true worth.

Ode to Alexandria

Alexandria, what tomes'
intense groans you evoke
from man's memory, proud nest
of the best the ancients spoke.

They covered science, the gods,
how fate plods—what you preserved
was the past's glory, which now
into sand's brow has since swerved.

Lost to all time, had you stood,
Serapeum, would our schools
not still be teaching the scrolls
whose rolls lined your walls? Mind drools!

Your days have sorely dimmed: sight
sees no more light from *Khem*'s isle
Pharos with fire's beam and ring
announcing *land near* with style.

There stood Ptolemies' bright gem,
pliant stem of writings' bloom
swaying with the winds of thought,
uplift wrought to rend man's gloom.

Warm Date [*(c)*]
[*Cywydd Deuair Hirion*]

A night's chill air notes each lure
that might give yen its tenure.
Need's demand is a demure
frost melted by imposture.

Man's Scrape [*(c)*]

How shall I dub these troubles
(bemoaned) whose bright ebb man dulls,
this scrape we're in the Spinner
(Fate) must nudge, that feet may stir?

Compel that no cue impede
trips to where truth has tarried:
follow every spark in full
and you'll find your plan ample.

The Condemned [*(c)*]

a noose dawns
    insidious
and kindly fuck
    this ruckus
to smithereens
    it smothers
my sail of fire's
    silver firs

which aspire to love's virus
still though will sought a lithe us
to tempt attempt more tortured
    intentions
    goal not assured

Turquoise by Day
[*Cyhydedd Fer*]

Turquoise by day, lapis by night—
the former with its blobs of white,
the latter with its points of light—
this flattened orb's a stalagmite
in the dark cave of space, a blight
on the stark calm of the void's plight
in having only us to right
the wrongs of nature. Crisp insight
is needed. But instead, man's might
only undermines the upright,
turns truth's diamond into graphite,
like a pre-Moses Canaanite,
making day a feeble nightlight.

We are the baby of the sky,
no more: stillborn, our throats are dry
from questioning exactly why
we must eat the *crust* of the pie
and leave the rest to vultures. Eye
of newt and toe of frog we'll try—
anything, lest our alibi
be compromised. Our efforts buy

no copper setting for the sun
nor silver setting for the one
whose star-points wink (where once was none,
if science be believed). They've won!
the spirits of ennui, who's fun
is tripping up thought's little run
of finding things to overcome
that won't be missed (such as reason).

Freestanding Byr a Thoddaid [*(c)*]

Assail tidy solitude. In lush warmth
shall mirth now be valued
or hot as bed, how tea is brewed
once night's chill turf has been curfewed.

Appeal to Self [*(c)*]

O reason, please arise now: piles
of tasks contrive to seek scant aisles.
Show moderation: aim, then run, hell-bent.
Who'll bite? Foresight, for one.

The 'Cramped' Present [*(c)*]

As Plato says, the present—most fleeting—
must float away, potent
yet dark, like space, one's fate latent
within its womb, the eye night sent.

Only what lasts glows, frozen—crystallized—
across it all, pollen
grown to flower, grant fallen
at our feet; picked up; eaten.

Blessing's Might [*(c)*]

Take to wing, blessing: be all sound
a while, to be one whole tie bound
for better, free but around, calming stress,
claiming stray thoughts' playground.

Spell for the New Paradigm (A Satire) [*~(c)*]

The outer world, that rarely deigns
to note my lot *or* my quatrains,
stumbles, lost, nay ambles lanes—avenues—
that will bruise the tall brains.

And so this charm: crouch; look harmless;
ply your *coy fool* ploy, nor confess
full value; urge feel of largesse—act lean.
Be seen a wreck: feckless.

Then shall blessings (thy shoal, o bliss)
from heaven course (firm heave, no kiss).
It's *sky* bears fruit, *not* trees' backs. Axis *up*,
thy cup awaits: make piss!

Love's Appeal [*(c)*]
[*Cywydd Llosgyrnog*]

Eye follows show if all's unsure.
Need air seem lithe under some lure
        Love's enduring levees draw?
Caressing truth, care sang it right:
Soon came wan limbs sunk in moonlight,
        Tender might to dare my awe.

Fiddler's Hymn

Ah ta hear the drone o' the pipes
in the ring of the G from swipes
        of me bow, that cares ta call
the music of a warlike heart
from peaceful strains of ancient art,
        the part that it plays for all.

It's calling when I think the tones
that make the melody and drones
      are loans from a far-off time.
The music's feelings bridge the span
of ages since these notes began
      better than a pantomime.

Visions of heather, river, wood
that flourished where both bad and good
      ancestors stood I can see.
Air rings of graces of gaunt days
and pathos spawned by evil's ways
      in the lays they sing to me.

O magic thing of wood and gut
and horsehair through which the sounds strut
      in a glut of bloodly thrill,
serenely ears become engrossed
ta hear past ages' conjured ghost,
      an' I toast they *ever* will.

Bran's and Krishna's Flute

Maker of calls I cannot make,
my lips being too glib to take
      the proper shape when they blow,
how plaintively your cries caress
the ear and calm the heart's distress:
      what blessing's boon you bestow!

Smoother of nerves in peace and strife,
big brother to the tinkly fife,
      you uplift life by your flight!
With throbbing pulse or pure clear tone
you laugh, you cry, you trill, you moan
      with a lonely, fragile might.

Wind in the reed, or bird in trees,
your music is a gentle breeze:
      you please us with sifted air.
Speak to the ages, fair-voiced thing:
say to them, by the song you sing,
      "Soul take wing and shun despair!"

From the Fallen

I did not see the end of day:
some shrapnel took my soul away,
      out of man's fray to hell's fold.
Yet knowing, I'd have not hung back
nor bequeathed others, in my lack,
      death's honest tack to behold.

Better one be remembered well
and told of fondly in song's spell
      than dwell in dark vales of shame.
My effort was by duty drawn
and spent itself—love's willing pawn—
      for honor and not mere name.

Celebrate not *my* driven choice,
to which these lines give fervent voice:
      rejoice for what souls my death
has kept preserved through battle's grind
who freedom's triumph hope to find,
      bought with mind and blood and breath.

Near Srebrenica
[*Clogyrnach*]

Orange the sun's departing show
colorless the ridge's shadow
for this valley's night

will have no more light
than the bright
searchlight's glow

A depression outlined in earth
gapes from just having given birth
to that which explains
the region's dark stains
left by pains
of great dearth

A strong scent pervades the still calm
opposite of a healing balm
unsavory stench
telling tales that wrench
hearts to clench
soothing psalm

Something stirs out beyond the beams
a gentle yelping that redeems
the chill that descends
where a north wind wends
from the ends
of man's dreams

A captain of artillery
asks of his guide if it might be
what has just been found
here beneath the ground
that the sound
seeks to see

Scavengers? No: they belong *here.*
Their masters . . . there! A creeping tear
cuts short his reply
as earth heaves a sigh
knowing why
dogs stay near

Myrddin's Song Sung Before Gwenddoleu

In cross-hallowed halls, the south sits
dissembling, twisting things through lips'
wrinkled care, their cause
needled by new laws
whose curt clause can crack whips.

By Lugh, Light of the gods, do we
beyond the Wall, still fierce and free,
oppose chains and choose
crisp battle's bare bruise
lest we lose wisdom's key.

In Praise of Rhydderch Hael of Strathclyde [*(c)*]

Sane is courage that sows increase:
a tough stride's pace to face strewed peace
forsaking fierce kin:
eyed, let daylight in
so that sin seethe to cease.

Video Killed the Radio Star
[*Rhupunt*]

Insipid air
is everywhere,
insistent stare
      of the mundane.
It's trampled down
the dapper clown
of chance renown
      that was man's brain.

To modernize
the ill-earned prize
for silly eyes
      would seem a waste.
Incessant tries
at compromise
make butterflies
      by glass encased.

The forms remain
and forge a strain
of farmers' wain
      to be ignored.
It plods along
through odds' old throng
is what is wrong
      with that accord.

Today's ill song
by pill or bong
      becomes a lord.
Little is left
whose lilt and heft
      can be restored.

I'll entertain
the winter train
      of my *own* fall
and catch no laughs
from hatched giraffes
      in my lone hall.

Welsh Measures Allowed the Chief Bard

[See also page 120]

Current Decline of Mind

[Gwawdodyn, lineated in a modern way]

Spoiled is the term
that springs to mind
    when asked
why
    when tasked
with thinking
    moderns grind
shimmering teeth
    then need to unwind
to recover wits
    whose tongues have dined
on platitudes
    in place of reason
    led
to their bed of lies
    by direction
of bald political correction
    a quest not
for meaning
    once begun

Where Were You, Poet, When Oppression Dawned? [*(c)*]
[*Gwawdodyn*]

Cauldron-born of Ceridwen—carpenter
of song!—stir now, voicing starry yen
to see sun's portal of hope open:
free feats' Luck today from fate's locked den!

The Head's Predicament
[*Cyhydedd Naw Ban*]

Odd anyone could get heads to stick
on bodies such as these, where the trick
is to appease the trapeze fabric
to where it thinks you share its rubric
that it's all molecules time's mules kick,
not notions, and nothing is epic.

There is no greater pain-in-the-neck
than that round little ludicrous speck
making a body's life one spent wreck
by misdirecting it on some trek
after abstract facts it fain would check,
expecting flesh to just genuflect.

Said bloated head needs a neck that's stout
to hold it up as it bobs about,
boss to angels in its high hideout,
princely perch till earth's lurch asserts clout,
tells it how to hang and when to pout,
leading it by hand into its snout.

*[Composed as a satire against a rude rival poet: after hearing it the bastard found himself
compelled by circumstances to move out of town before the following week's workshop!]*

Cheap Seats Under Apple Boughs [~*(c)*]
or
I've Run Out of Give, Are You With Me?

Hind soon assays primed senses' pyramid
here amid alley cans and trances
indicative of, indigenous to
zoo-like circumflex circumstances
empiricism demands Kansas
take note of. Make a votive muck—of time,
of tomb, beaten vellum—but not of Luck:
that's where bucks stop in this synopsis
for a tourist's view of the newness,
this 'give' our negative run got us.

Under the apple tree are we, arrows
rise but stick in the thicket thickly,
allowing us a breather to re-think
this thing, this stray stink sense, this shaky
perilous-feral-fuss-for-low-fee:
I've run out of give, are you with me?

[Composed the night my best friend died (unbeknownst to me), whose humor this reflects]

Own Your Karma

What's intended, sincerely thought—believed—
is heaved onto the karma pile, caught
in retribution's cyclic onslaught
that seeks to teach us but leaves untaught
those who think that fate's guards can be bought,
or by whom scapegoats are always sought
on whom to press blame for what fate brought:
this, man's greatest demon, brings to naught
all the pleasures for which he has fought.

There But For the Grace of Will [*(c)*]

Speak, folly! Impress me: my purse mends
nothing here. My tear welled in me tends
to hide as my pained toe heeds, impends
upon draped humans shaped how mush ends
when it feeds folly's seeds. Foul ooze sends
a message to my nose, imposing
further constraint: fear, the recast ring
of doubt, is thus called. Want is balding,
aged beyond whim, like jade bound humming
past a stone grave, pissed: a stain, grieving.
Shadow's hands bend one to face sunlight,
dim place hope fled. Impulse, hop a flight
for better days: man's fire betrayed night,
made its eyelid mud, want's load a might
that makes us wince at pain's deep insight.

World War One [*(c)*]

Lives, ebullient—snuffed, low, visible
in the rocky place—neither cope, lull,
nor stir: a mat of consumed cattle,
death by cunning guns' naïve evil,
traded for feet, an inching beetle
strewing men in flowers and fennel,
each clawed yard worth a thousand hardships,
thousands lost to breath. Damn the ethics
of those—miles behind—whose scant antics
constitute their 'astute' nudge through sticks
pointing at empty space, death's basics
dictating how the clock addict ticks,
seeks a new fate from the same matrix.

The Duke of Wellington by Goya

I had never studied his visage—
eyes half focused, of noble carriage,
soft narrow mouth, raised brows, tamed plumage,
hyper-attentive ear (a message
destined for its future), privilege
written on him, yet without wastage
of self-flattery, I would allege,
serious enough that tutelage
took, allowing sense and forced usage
to lift mind beyond skin and package
to the lit source of faith and courage
in self, in men, giving him the edge
over vanity's hollow peerage
on the other side of war's thin hedge.

The Credentialed Poet [*(c)*]

O lofty one, oft published in ooze
and Oz, I'm all ears. Gnaw, dismal ruse!
Parade that can't stir beyond curfews
in stirrup-crowds, you sate or ape crews
whose ears are stuffed. His oars rest, o Muse,
while I *drink* your song! Healed rancor soothes,
bound to pasts' vain bandit posts of news,
fixed at a mast, focused to amuse.
Know you these mysteries' aim, star-eyed
club-eared voice a clue bared? Eve sighed
when Adam conjured. Honed meek nudge, ride
round in your small corral while allied
dust cloud's need, a herd, stay clods and hide
waiting for a giant's grand landslide
to lure their hooves from home and bromide.

Words to the Not-So-Wise

I tell you, man,
      if you haven't learned
to laugh at yourself,
      then you're patterned
to live from rage to rage,
      taciturned
only by death,
      and poorly lanterned:
humor lets in light
      where pride gets burned.

Bill Hickock: Ode to a Life Fulfilled
[A descendent of Wild Bill himself]

Humor and civility spilled—spruced up—
into the cup life held to be filled.
Effortless! like a mess left unstilled
in that quest to which the bless'd have thrilled
(that few have noticed and fewer quilled).

He offered his dry red wine unchilled.

While late in years he seemed almost gilled,
'twas such a form his hammer anvil'd
on space-time as can't be daffodil'd
nor grown over (though gone) for he tilled
fields on which eternal truths have drilled.

He grew grain our memory has milled.

Leave him as he left us: well jonquil'd
knowing it's but for a time we're billed.

This round, he was a claret, well swilled.

To the Poet

Of all tasks poetry clasps none
      outweighs
ways to unearth gnosis:
      worth hard-won!
precious beyond
golden tined
      diction.

Misfit [*(c)*]

I am loud enacting
      mild nocturnes
resist rain
      though I drink from cisterns
must have
      what is hidden in caverns
am adroit or else
      the mad returns

quake not who care for me
      the æons
pile up anyway
      a playpen yawns
if love begins
      a file of bygones
rather than bitters
      or other wrongs

if I've left the room
      then ruminate
on absence
      or on the insensate
task   let no
      opportunity skate
ether-eyed regrets end up
      third rate

Under the Eaves

Life, why have you left me in this time
when English usage is in decline
(called archaic) and the paradigm
most on which our delving wits must dine
is one dragged from beneath pungent slime?

Dried out skies still starlit sparkle
         no more
         in mire
rooted and unmagical
decay spawned as dreams delusional
in content and intent meant to lull
to sleep each grain of truth still supple.

Here beside the turning of the leaves,
why'm I left crouching under the eaves?

Sunlight on Water

The sea angles down
        but edges up
into the air
        element it cut
off at the feet
        filling the great rut
the world is which is now a cup
        brimming
boar among beasts rooting out the muck

Insidious moisture infiltrates
atmosphere as it evaporates
disguises itself as air
        creates
weather everywhere
        and winter's aches
and it will until the world abates

In the Style
of
Dark Ages Britain

Based on the thorough analysis of Aneirin's poetry presented in *The Gododdin of Aneirin: Text and Context from Dark-Age North Britain*, edited by John T. Koch, who reconstructs the original Brittonic version and comments on its sound figures.

Mind-gate: Solve (et Coagula)

Sand between my toes,
toes my tentacles . . .

tentacles searching . . .

searching out the eye,
aye, of this pale storm
storm-ridden within,
yet calmer than beyond its rim

Quick, burst these fierce clouds
clods are governed by
by battering gusts,
gusts disgust must spew,
spew against all four
of the four winds due.

Enlightened Hippy's Quandary in Dismal Times

How we relished vision's catalyst
that seeped inside each fresh anti-statist
bent cerebrum seeking freedom's twist—
man's chance to demystify the missed.

A round peg in these square times, I abhor
the risk of that fading fast into folklore:
am I truly the lone stevedore
unloading rich ships on the sea floor
sunk there by the collective ear's closed door?

Who knows how the phrase *who knows* gets glossed
once the warmth to wait has turned to frost.
Secrets of such strength are worth great cost.

My Favorite Decade

My favorite decade
      is one that hasn't happened yet
one that stars muscle cars
      better than a Corvette
and a trend in music's bent
      marking an end to a dull set
that was started many a moon ago
      by some marmoset
with nice hair that had savoir faire
      (for a pet)
and peed on Johnny Carson's head
      (on a bet)
and thus was given unlimited
      access to the net
so as to catch the fallen fallacy
      of the coquette
in a trap called an app
      and warm leatherette

My favorite decade
      existed in the distant past
beyond the vast dinosaurs
      and the primal forest's rasp
that filed the world's corners off
      and the contrast
between individuals
      and their bombast
long before modern war
      made man morassed
in this whory gory glory
      with which we have been tasked
at the behest of the least best
      our natures ask
one whose trends grace sends
      as it wends through the cast
of the play that this world is
      but will it last

My favorite decade
      I must make on my own
for the people won't do it
      (nor leave me the hell alone)
so it's up to my fervent guess
      what's dull and what is shone
in the gleam of an outer eye
      (that being why it's grown)
and the case I must make for it
      (and win) is the syndrome
out of which was spawned
      what now dawns—what'll've flown
in this test flight of happiness
      that's tossed the dog a bone
in the hopes it would chase it
      in hopes it hadn't known
that that white thing was the tail end
      of a cyclone

Sardonic's Gleam

dismal the city seems
      in sunlight
less unlike than blight would be
      the pale dreams
contentment spans
      yet zen foe to phonemes
of the heart
      whose pale art
         imitates
      wings

in the mists of morning
      nature asserts herself
here so aloof
      yet where there's proof truth hurts
cold cringes
      at the binges of converts
to the concrete
      from the frail
         greens
      of deserts

Yes, but Where Did I Leave My Mind?

It is only an inconsiderable mess
this tidbit of stress the world's been under
since its insidious loss of wonder
at the architectural marvel the stars were
once it was made out they as little matter
as individuals as do we since larger
fields are afoot of a meaning lesser
even than the mote on a throw of dice cups in amber
frozen long ago in the pose of a dancer
in this ballet of the melodramatic whir
that has danced quiet agonies to peals of thunder
since Adam was a schoolboy and earth much cooler

then than now and anyhow we didn't fool 'er
she sank into the gold where we couldn't tool 'er
and contemplated giving back the rib as a spoiler
what was it that was her name
night
or something similar . . .

Sewn as with Wire

Shall my spear
of speech pierce
      your spirit's peace anew?

Sentence passed,
repentance cast,
      you'd still argue—
mind's blockage
is its own stoppage
      when in a stew.

Hence tongue stays still,
though from love's will
      I owe it you.

Would we might
frolic in light,
be all bright
      and gay,
make minds' meeting last
as fleeting past
      falls away
with us standing outside our rooms
      in a common hallway
but that's not how it is today
      for the seams
      between our dreams
are stitched in wire
      barbed with dismay.

Intermeshed Strands of Thought's Force

We are all sorcerers
whose source of power stirs
      will's vapors from mere whims.
The times hid from thought
what thinking wrought
      but we're caught in its limbs.

Confession

I do not *write* poetry: I *compose* it.
It's just that while a poem is in transit
to others' mouths, one must apply one's wit
to arranging the words that flow forth so they fit
comfortably on a page, to become the bit
that reins in someone else's speech, to benefit
from this talent I was born with in my kit—
which also includes that of fiddling twit
in a pinch, and of course thinker of merit
(unrecognized but real), my mind being well lit.

At least I don't have to worry they'll audit
my finances anytime soon, since the chit
I earn from such talents (once treasured) does credit
to Diogenes by imitating his quaint habit
of unabashed homelessness, surely a gambit
to garner attention and show the deficit
he rated the world as. Indeed what I posit
as answers to problems the world's great flaws emit—
from which we may *not* run away like a rabbit
but rather must weather wherever we sit—
will surely earn me plaudit after plaudit . . .
      except I'm not
      anyone
      you can edit.

Reluctant Optimist

Alas, let us join this drudgerous day
which no mere glittering night
of lust's spent might
      might allay
the weight of if man's crass fate has its way
for the thoughts we bring near
seep clear
      into the clay.

Miscreant Mimicry
[Inspired by Dylan Thomas's "Fern Hill"]

you can forgive the glintings of moved steel-like
passages in pieces pounded into blight
of the long haul boasted of beyond insight
or one or more of things lore means gathered tight
tied up in a ball as if they were alright
with their withering calm allayed sunwise by night

still flesh to mill about must leave its lean pallet
water sparkling savory in the spilled day yet—pleasant
miscreant mimicry seeking to become ably hep
to the short stick grabbed at quick by some Imhotep
hidden amongst grasses with the adders and wet
as will admit clods' softened heads as an asset

very astute winnings this as he sings to eat
and eats to sing heart taking wing for the wild feat
of flying solo through so low a life elite
but mis-established tablet from the high heap
after Babel and the dense yet winsome well of the fleet
and hip that hop on all threes not lame but deep

A Twist on Cyrch Gymeriad

coolness itself—
self's self-centered
interred-in-guilt
gilt mound of earth
worth naught mention—
shunned me still

till hummed this page
rage has as nave
engraved tranquil

quill we call work
as we 'work' others
(udders dripping
gripping kindness)
mind nests beside
your bedside skill

swill (in these airs
arrogance stirs)
stars' mute trickle

How to Leave the World

entrenched
in the calm
of palm-severed sand
land's insects inland from my hand

I watched as the sun
got caught in the hatch
at sunset and it
opened up a latch

long locked
and led me

down its garden path
into advent
of nightingales

you laugh

yet a sigh now chimes the air
where riff-raff
legions
of aggravants
had signaled wrath

pen prepare
a proper bark
for the pond

to leave the world
both singing
and songed

Earthquake Weather

Arch, this still wind
wind stirred from sloth.

Sloth with bared teeth
teethes on regrets,
regrets nothing.

Thing of frail bits
bits of fear shed,
shadow-tilted,
it sees days as already wilted.

Dim prospects slew
a slew of breaths
breath's source embraced,
braced the days with.

With no blade, hand
hand-carved this void
void of its torch:
torch-stand jolted
when the hills' deeper bent revolted.

We of Good Cheer Endure

injection of joie de vivre into the mix
meant as a fix where mounting tensions seethe
contradicts events yet does not deceive
for it is *us* not *time* such thoughts relieve

it was in the pearled pulchritude of youth's madness
unleashed on levity with its horse riderless
that life ingested me and I it to address
not how the highbrow might bow to mind's largesse
but molding mind into the kind
        destined to find truth's fastness

now without patronage how can it last
since under poverty's wheels I am stuck fast
but why worry
a springy durmast
        will I be
in life's wee storm
being one born
        neither king nor outcast
but a wielder of words
to the vast herds
        doubt's seeds have amassed

Th-th-th-that's all, folks.